8-31

MILTON'S ELISIONS

by Robert O. Evans, 1919-

UNIVERSITY OF FLORIDA PRESS / GAINESVILLE, 1966

EDITORIAL COMMITTEE

Humanities Monographs

T. WALTER HERBERT, *Chairman*
Professor of English

G. PAUL MOORE
Professor of Speech

CHARLES W. MORRIS
Professor of Philosophy

REID POOLE
Professor of Music

C. A. ROBERTSON
Professor Emeritus of English

MELVIN E. VALK
Associate Professor of German

AUBREY L. WILLIAMS
Graduate Research Professor
of English

ACKNOWLEDGMENTS

Much of the material that follows appeared originally, in somewhat different form, in my University of Florida doctoral dissertation, "The Theory and Practice of Metrical Elision from Chaucer to Milton, with special emphasis on Milton." The primary thesis of that paper was to demonstrate that poetic elision was a deliberate prosodic practice, consisting of a series of devices that were traditionally passed on from one generation of poets to another. The purpose of this monograph, to explain as fully as possible just what Milton's practices were, is different.

I am deeply indebted to Professor Ants Oras, who directed my dissertation and generously contributed advice for this work, without whose kind encouragement and astute assistance this monograph could never have been written. I owe another kind of debt to my wife whose patient encouragement, especially through the long evenings in which I gathered the material, has been invaluable. I am also grateful to the University of Kentucky Research Fund and to President John

W. Oswald, for kindly granting me a summer research fellowship which permitted me to set aside the time necessary to complete the work. Finally I am deeply indebted to the Graduate School of the University of Florida, both for the time and patience spent on my education and for making possible the publication of this monograph.

ROBERT O. EVANS

Lexington, Kentucky
1966

AUTHOR'S NOTE

For reasons which will become clear to the reader this study is based on the "New Edition" of the *Poetical Works of John Milton*, edited by H. C. Beeching, "with Translations of the Italian, Latin and Greek Poems from the Columbia University Edition and a Reader's Guide by W. Skeat" (London: Oxford University Press, 1938, first printed in 1904).

CONTENTS

The measure is *English* Heroic Verse without Rime. . . . Not without cause therefore some both *Italian* and *Spanish* Poets of prime note have rejected Rime both in longer and shorter Works, as have also long since our best *English* Tragedies, as a thing of it self, to all judicious eares, triveal and of no true musical delight; which consists only in apt Numbers, fit quantity of Syllables, and the sense variously drawn out from one Verse to another.

—from a note "The Verse," added by Milton in 1668 to the remaining copies of the first edition of *Paradise Lost.*

1. SOME CONCEPTS
AND DEFINITIONS

Metrical or poetic elision is a specialized technical term that does not mean exactly what its etymology may suggest, particularly to one whose introduction to the subject comes through the classical languages. In this context it is strictly a prosodic term, though a qualifying adjective like *metrical* or *poetic* is not really sufficient to distinguish the technical meaning from the ordinary, dictionary one. There are good reasons why certain confusions exist about the term, for the language of prosody is not at all a scientific, exact language, like that of chemistry, for instance, where the terms are clear and well defined—to be memorized by all the practitioners of the art. On the contrary, prosodists (or perhaps metrists) and poets, those who practice prosody, are inclined to invent their language as they go along, often with considerable scorn for prior definitions. Even a hasty examination of the metrical handbooks of, say, Italy, France, or Spain will exhibit areas of violent contradiction in terminology, caused in the main by one writer's referring to a certain thing by a particular technical term while another may mean something quite different by the same words, sometimes even something diametrically opposite. Thus, it is important from the beginning to be extremely careful of definitions and the concepts on which they rest.

Thus elision, which is sometimes defined as the "cutting out" of something in words, is concerned with the special study of what happens to syllables in the flow of speech and, by extension, to what happens to syllables in the flow of the poetic line. It is furthermore concerned with the very nature of the syllable itself, a concept so simple every child can grasp it almost at once yet so complicated even the experts cannot agree about it. As A. Rosetti has said: "La définition et la délimitation de la syllabe n'aurait pas suscité autant de discussions contradictoires, si l'on s'était adressé dès le début à la réalité objective, en consultant

1

l'inscription de la voix parlée. Mais l'on a procédé autrement. . . ."[1]

There are indeed at least five theories about the nature of the syllable that find adherents today: the Sievers theory that a syllable is characterized by a separate puff of breath, the Saussure that the defining characteristics are an opening and closing of the oral cavity, the Tomas theory concerning the single peak of sonority, Grammont's theory of muscular tension, and De Groot's idea that a syllable is a rhythmical grouping. With so much trouble defining what we are talking about, no wonder there is confusion when we try to describe particular things that happen to the syllable under specified conditions. In a study of syllables *elision* is the generic term referring to the cutting out or slurring of a syllable in the flow of speech. In its broadest sense *elision* includes everyday speech contractions, and sometimes peculiarities of a poet's private pronunciation which may be dialectal or idiosyncratic. This is the sense in which the term has been used since the Renaissance, by writers like Bentley, Guest, and others.[2] Their meaning is undoubtedly an extension of what English scholars learned from Greek grammar, where *elision*, strictly speaking, is "the expulsion of a short vowel before a word beginning with a vowel"; it may or may not be indicated in the Greek MSS, but in any case "it seems to have occurred in speaking."[3] Robert Bridges objects to the use of the word in its extended meaning on the grounds that it is too broad and that it is an inaccurate description of certain phonetic happenings: "Since the word elision signifies the 'cutting out' there would seem an impropriety in using it to describe the condition of syllabic vowels which are not truly elided or cut out of the pronunciation."[4] There is a hint in this statement that Bridges thinks there is a sort

---

1. A. Rosetti, *Sur la Théorie de la Syllabe* (The Hague: Mouton & Co., 1959), 11. (This pamphlet is No. IX of the series *Janua Linguarum*, printed originally in Bucharest in 1958.)

2. Ants Oras, *Milton's Editors and Commentators from Patrick Hume to Henry John Todd* (Oxford, 1931) and Edwin Guest, *A History of English Rhythms*, 2 vols. (London, 1838).

3. H. W. Smyth, *A Greek Grammar for Colleges* (New York, 1920), 23.

4. Robert Bridges, *Milton's Prosody* (Oxford, 1921), 9.

of elision which is not really a cutting out or syllabic reduction of sounds. In fact one of Bridges' major contributions to the theory of elision is that there may be elisions (as poetic devices) that are really nothing more than a highly imaginative fiction, places in the verse where no real reduction of sounds occurs but where the mind, accustomed to the poetic device, reacts as if elision had actually taken place. In addition to this fictive elision Bridges attempts to demonstrate that the phenomenon differs from that in Greek because in English it is permissive. That is, it may or may not happen, depending on the meter. In Greek it seems always to have occurred in speech, though the MSS that have come down to us are highly inconsistent about indicating it with an apostrophe. Bridges' theories are based on his own observations and on his reading of Milton aloud. Their great merit is that they free us from the necessity of explaining all cases where an apparent extrametrical syllable seems to exist in terms of complete and real phonetic foreshortenings. What Bridges is really arguing is that elision is a conscious poetic device rather than always an actual phonetic phenomenon.

His objection to the term *elision* may be a sound one, but in its place he proposes that we substitute that Latin term *synaloepha*. It is, he says, "commonly used by correct grammarians."[5] It is— in grammars—though the Greek term *crasis* is found more frequently, but perhaps Bridges is attempting to substitute a term too limited in its meaning, for *synaloepha* has come to refer especially to the dropping of a final vowel before a word beginning with a vowel, semivowel, or aspirate. Bridges is right about his Greek, however, for there *synaloepha* meant the blending together of two adjacent vowels by elision, crasis, synizesis—sometimes indicated in the spelling of the MS and sometimes not, but always pronounced. What has happened is that, in the borrowing from Greek to Latin to English, the two terms *elision* and *synaloepha* have exchanged meanings; the more general has become the more particular and incidentally the less familiar. *Synaloepha* is not commonly understood except by specialists; *elision*, on the other hand, is known to nearly everybody, and there is usually a

5. *Ibid.*

3

good, practical definition of it in our handbooks: "*Elision:* The omission of a part of a word for ease of pronunciation, for euphony, or to secure a desired rhythmic effect. This is most often accomplished by the omission of a final vowel as 'th' orient' for 'the orient' but *elision* also occurs between syllables of a word as 'ne'er' for 'never.' "[6]

6. Thrall and Hibbard, *A Handbook to Literature* (New York, 1936), 140.

2. COMMON VARIETIES
OF ELISION

Though elision is a poetic device, all poets are not equally skilled in its use; therefore, some poets may overwork one variety or another while others develop a more balanced practice. Moreover, it can be noted, in a few cases it is not possible to classify a particular elision at all; that is, some elisions seem to fit the conditions of more than one type. However, by observation and grouping, the common or traditional types may be isolated; these account for more than 95 per cent of all the elisions in English verse between Chaucer and Milton. Others, that may be thought of as exceptions, are mostly quite easy to describe, though a few occur so infrequently that it is not possible to be sure whether we are observing a rare variety of elision or a real extrametrical syllable (sometimes perhaps an unintentional one).

In *Milton's Prosody* Bridges finds eight varieties of elision. While there is little reason to quarrel with his careful observations, these classifications are somewhat untrustworthy because they are based on his private, self-taught notions of phonetics. His classifications are so complex, and often so unsound, that they have been severely criticized. Some writers, however, have made considerable use of them. For example, S. Ernest Sprott reduces Bridges' eight varieties to two inclusive categories—contractions and the synaloepha of vowels.[1] But for purposes of comparison it is desirable to break down the categories further than Sprott does. Practically all of the common elisions in English verse from Chaucer to Milton may be grouped into the following varieties: (1) hypermonosyllables; (2) elision over liquids and nasals, and sometimes sibilants, where they are intervocalic; (3) elision by synaloepha of a final vowel preceding a word beginning with a vowel, semivowel, or aspirate; (4) elision between contiguous vowels (either a common speech situation

1. S. E. Sprott, *Milton's Art of Prosody* (Oxford: Basil Blackwell, 1953), 54-98. I refer to chapter VI, "Supernumerary Syllables and Elision."

or a sort of poetic, fictional diphthongization); (5) speech contractions themselves; (6) elision by considering a final inflection as non-syllabic (usually *-es, -ed, -eth*, possibly *-ing*, and in some cases a final liquid or nasal); (7) *rarely*, those few special items where the principle is not readily discernible. As Milton does not indulge in the last category, we may omit further consideration of it here; speech contractions are also too well understood to require attention.

HYPERMONOSYLLABLES: Bridges explains these as words which undergo what he calls a *-y* or *-w* glide, but this explanation is phonetically very unsatisfactory. In fact hypermonosyllables are that class of words whose pronunciation in English might historically be either monosyllabic or disyllabic, words like *heaven* or *power*. For example, in *Il Penseroso* Milton writes:

Whose pow/er hath / a true / consent (line 95)

The meter indicates that *power* in the above line is a disyllable. But in *Paradise Lost* it is quite consistently a monosyllable, as it often is in Spenser and Shakespeare:

His ut/most *power* / with ad/verse *power* / oppos'd (I.103)

ELISION OVER LIQUIDS AND NASALS: When a liquid, nasal, or sometimes a sibilant is intervocalic, elision may occur, usually of the vowel preceding the consonant. Generally neither vowel is stressed, but even when one is, elision may still take place; as with Milton's monosyllabic use of the word *spirit*. An example of an elision of the vowel preceding a liquid might be:

As one / who long / in pop/*u*lous Cit/y pent (IX.445)

Bridges considers this to be a real elision probably pronounced *pop'lous*, and Wyld reports the similar loss of an unstressed vowel in *abslate* for *absolute* in 1641.[2] In Milton this could occur even between words.

In some cases it is not possible to state with certainty which vowel is elided:

2. H. C. Wyld, *A History of Modern Colloquial English* (New York, 1937), 408.

6

Not dis/tant far / from thence / a mur/*muring* sound
(IV.453)

Here we find an intervocalic liquid; Bridges with his greater number of categories calls this elision according to the "Rule of R." It seems very likely that Milton considered the elision to concern the initial vowel, with a pronunciation something like *murm'ring* in mind, but it is just conceivable that the following vowel could undergo elision, *murmur'n*.

ELISION BY SYNALOEPHA: Strictly speaking, synaloepha is the suppression of hiatus (that is, vowel clash) between words by the cutting out or partial reduction of a vowel, rather than suppression of vowel clash by the insertion of a hiatus-filler (the favorite textbook example, *an adder*). Commonly words ending in a vowel, usually prepositions and articles, elide the final vowel of the first word before a word beginning with another vowel, semi-vowel, or aspirate:

Above / th'*A*o/nian Mount / while it / pursues (I.15)

(There is another elision in the third foot which should not be mistaken for an example of the variety under discussion.) It should be pointed out that few, if any, English poets are very consistent about indicating synaloepha orthographically. At one time they may spell both words fully when the meter indicates an elision; at another time they may write an apostrophe (e.g., *th'*) where none is intended. In Milton such diacritical marks might be the fault of his amanuensis, but in fact they occur often enough in English poetry to lead us to suspect that the poet himself was often responsible.

ELISION BETWEEN CONTIGUOUS VOWELS: Two different kinds of elision fall under this category. First, we should consider common speech situations. For instance, the suffix *-tion*, originally disyllabic, underwent a sound change, the result of which made it monosyllabic. In Marlowe's and Shakespeare's time the suffix is generally used monsyllabically, though Renaissance poets, particularly Spenser, often reserved the license to revert to an older pronunciation when it suited their purposes:

7

> Thus grace/less holds / he dis/puta/ti-on
> (*The Rape of Lucrece*, 246)

In view of such practices, when a Renaissance poet uses the suffix monosyllabically, we may consider it an example of elision, because the possibility of an archaic, disyllabic pronunciation was always open to him, even if he did not exactly have it in mind while writing. But whether a prosodist should count *-tion* suffixes in his statistical tabulations is quite another matter. As Shakespeare, for example, usually used this suffix monosyllabically and as that was the current pronunciation, it would seem desirable not to clutter our tabulations with a large number of *-tion* instances, even though Shakespeare might have thought of each one of them as a matter of poetic elision (as unlikely as that may be).

In some other cases we seem more likely to be dealing with a poetic device than a linguistic circumstance. For example, in the suffix *-ience*, probably disyllabic in the seventeenth century as it is in American speech today, the first syllable is very short. It does not require much imaginative license for a poet to consider the entire suffix to be monosyllabic. In fact, the initial vowel need not actually disappear, or be reduced to a semivowel as it often is today, for a poet to treat the suffix as an elision. Examples occur frequently, as in *Samson Agonistes* for instance:

> Now of / my own / exper/*ien*ce, not / by talk (line 188)

NON-SYLLABIC INFLECTIONS: In English there is a tendency for final inflections to lose their syllabic quality and sometimes eventually to disappear. Thus, *thinkest* becomes *thinkst*, and *doeth* (at least in most dialects) becomes *doth* before it gives way to *does*. Again *passed* has long since been monosyllabic, though we are all familiar with the conscious archaism with which some poets, notably Spenser, reattribute syllabic quality to the inflection. In modern printing this is often indicated by an accent mark over the inflectional vowel. A close study of poetry indicates that the matter was not entirely one of linguistic change; it was often a poetic device. Perhaps it arose at a time when the pro-

8

nunciation of the inflections was unstable, and poets—noting an instability in common speech—took poetic advantage and elided whenever the meter offered a suitable opportunity. For example, in *Paradise Lost* Milton wrote:

He trust/ed to / have e/qual'*d* the / most High (I.40)

The inflection in the fourth foot no longer has any syllabic value. However, Milton often rehabilitated the inflections in adjectives and participles (though not in finite verb forms), as he did with *thron-ed* and *fix-ed.* He did not do this with *trusted* (in line 40, above) because it is a finite verb form and also because the coincidence of two dentals would make a monosyllabic pronunciation preposterous.

Not all poets used this device in the same fashion; some elided only certain inflections, while others preferred different ones. The loss of syllabic value in forms ending in *-ed* occurred early, and words ending with a non-syllabic inflection, the list of which is very long, were probably pronounced that way at the time Shakespeare and Milton wrote. Thus, it would not be desirable to consider all non-syllabic *-ed* forms as examples of poetic elision. It is much easier, and probably more accurate, to think of syllabic *-ed* as another device, a conscious archaism as it clearly was with Spenser.

With other inflections it is not always possible to ascertain whether a poet was simply writing a familiar idiom or whether he was constructing a poetic device. For instance, it is particularly hard for modern readers to recognize the inflection *-eth* (sometimes *-ith*) as a potential elision, though with Skelton and Wyatt particularly it was a genuine poetic device usually spelled with the vowel even when it was meant to be elided. Perhaps it is especially hard to recognize because it was an elision that was not carried forward through the sixteenth century. Somewhere between Wyatt and Surrey that inflection disappeared in the language of the poets and was replaced by the sibilant. And because we are familiar mostly with the elisions of the later poets (and then only the very common ones), we are likely to consider a non-syllabic occurrence of *-eth* to represent an extrametrical

9

syllable, even when that is not the case at all. The argument may be clinched by tracing that inflection through the Middle Scots poets, for there the sibilant replaced -*eth* much earlier, and we find the syllabic -*es* form, which was elidible in the same fashion that poets in the South used when they dealt with -*eth*.

The categories described above are based simply on observation of prosodic phenomena, rather than principles conceived and stated by Renaissance writers or critics. The writers themselves, with certain exceptions such as Ben Jonson who had a critical turn of mind, seldom discussed these devices, which were perhaps so commonplace to them that they felt little need to furnish explanations. Occasionally one rhetorician or another would incorporate some of the devices into his rhetorical scheme, usually it would seem in order to approach completeness. But the lack of discussion of these matters in Renaissance works certainly does not indicate that either the writers or the critics were in the dark about them. On the whole Italian critics were rather more voluble than English,[3] but even in England the devices are sometimes referred to as if they were matters of familiar knowledge. George Gascoigne, for example, wrote: "This poetical licence is a shrewde fellow, and couereth many faults in a verse; it maketh wordes longer, shorter, of mo sillables, of fewer, newer, older, truer, falser; and, to conclude, it turkeneth all things at pleasure, for example *ydone* for *done, adowne* for *downe, orecome* for *ouercome, tane* for *taken, power* for *powre, heauen* for *heaun.*"[4]

There is nevertheless some danger involved in any sort of classification, even that based on observation, for the poets themselves probably took no such pains but instead formed one elision after another by a process of analogy. That this was the primary method of formation seems to be indicated by the fact that the later a work the more complex are likely to be its elisions. I do not mean that later poets employed more categories

3. An excellent summary of the Italian position, with extensive quotations from Trissino, may be found in an article by George A. Kellogg, "Bridges' *Milton's Prosody* and Renaissance Metrical Theory," *PMLA* (March, 1953), 268-85.

4. G. Gregory Smith (ed.), *Elizabethan Critical Essays* (Oxford, 1904), I, 53-54.

10

but rather that their lists of elidible words are longer. But we cannot consider this evidence conclusive, for poets were under no orders to employ all the elisions they could conceive, nor even to elide at all. Moreover, a favorite word elided in one poem might not suit a poet in another, or simply because it was a poetic device he might tire of it and allow it to fall into neglect. Milton, for example, used feminine endings in abundance in his earlier poems, largely abandoned them in the first half of *Paradise Lost*, and turned to them again, though with considerable restraint, in the last half of that poem and in *Paradise Regained*, and finally, employed them in profusion again in *Samson Agonistes*. Then, in the eighteenth century the whole practice of poetic elision fell into disuse. Milton's editors, like Bentley, knew of the practice, of course, but largely condemned it.[5] Thelwall insisted that elidible syllables "should never in typography or utterance be superseded by the barbarous expedient of elision."[6] Writers and critics of the Renaissance would have thought this heresy.

5. Oras, 67.
6. Guest, I, 179.

3. JOHN MILTON'S PRACTICE

With Milton the syllabic tradition reaches its culmination. Accordingly, Milton is the most rewarding poet to examine with regard to these matters, but there is still another reason for directing our attention to him. More has been written about Milton's prosody than about the prosody of all the other English poets put together. Moreover, though much of the best thinking about prosodic problems has been accomplished by Milton scholars, much also has been written, and continues to be written, that is questionable. For example, F. T. Prince in 1954, arguing for a greater influence on Milton from the Italians than has hitherto been recognized—in a book that otherwise possesses many merits—flatly denies the existence of any prosodical schemes in Milton's versification governing the treatment of syllables. A study of the Italian models, he says, makes "unnecessary the construction of any such system of prosody as that which Robert Bridges attempted and which is generally considered indispensable by scholars."[1] Prince's chapter is confusing because he fails to keep separate the problems concerning accent and those dealing with the number of syllables in the verses, and accordingly issues a blanket denial that any such problems exist at all. The verse unit in Milton, and the Italians, he claims, was simply the line itself. But interesting as this theory is, it has not managed to persuade many writers. Seymour Chatman, in one of the most recent statements on the subject, says, "By distinguishing between scansion and metrical analysis, we may conceive of either performance, with or without scansional elision, without denying the *metrical* existence of elision at this point."[2] Indeed, if English poets had not been concerned with meter, and accordingly with the number of syllables within the line, English poetry could hardly have developed as it did. Moreover, Milton,

1. F. T. Prince, *The Italian Element in Milton's Verse* (Oxford, 1954), 139.
2. Seymour Chatman, *A Theory of Meter* (The Hague: Mouton & Co., 1965), 106.

no matter what his debt to the Italians (and it was large), drew his basic prosodic techniques from a strong English tradition.[3]

To begin with, when Milton began to compose *Paradise Lost*, he was faced, perhaps more acutely than anyone before him, with the problem of securing variation in the line. Having chosen to write in the orthodox metrical fashion, he largely solved this problem by employing devices that were ready to his hand. But he brought to his task such great genius and such an infinite and painstaking capacity for attention to fine detail that it became almost impossible for a lesser poet to emulate, much less equal, him.

Through the years so much has been written about Milton's prosody, and, since Robert Bridges, so much about his techniques of metrical elision, that it would be impossible to deal with all of it even briefly. Certain theories, however, require commentary, especially Bridges' which, despite all the controversy on the subject, remains the most important statement of Milton's practice, though it was by no means the first attempt to describe it.

ROBERT BRIDGES' THEORY: Bridges' final statements are to be found in the 1921 edition of *Milton's Prosody*, but if one traces his way through the earlier editions and reads Bridges' articles he will find that Bridges altered his position from time to time.[4] These changes led Prince to conclude that Bridges "had deep mental reservations concerning his method of analysis."[5] But the evidence does not quite support that implication. Bridges, a poet himself in what was perhaps a rather vulnerable position, who may have first stated his findings too hastily, was soundly attacked for his views and, as a result, never ceased his work of prosodical analysis. Moreover, Prince overstates his objections, as many of Bridges' critics had already done, and his conclusion that the English decasyllable (also called the iambic pentameter line) does not exist is untenable.

3. Robert Owen Evans, "The Theory and Practice of Poetic Elision from Chaucer to Milton, with special emphasis on Milton" (University of Florida dissertation, 1954). (Available in University of Michigan Microfilm series.)

4. Robert Bridges, "A Letter to a Musician on English Prosody," *The Musical Antiquary*, I (October, 1909), 13-27.   5. Prince, 136.

13

What Bridges did was scan the corpus of Milton's poetry very carefully listing all the seeming irregularities. Unfortunately he lived in an age when the Renaissance traditions had been so far forgotten that all situations involving metrical elision seemed to him, at first, to be irregularities, requiring either that one accept them as instances of extrametrical syllables or provide some sort of alternative explanation. Bridges chose to seek an answer to the questions that arose concerning the number of syllables in the line, and later he extended his analysis to include problems of accent and other matters. So far as Bridges' opinions of Milton's treatment of syllables are concerned, there is room for objection —but not to his methods. Bridges isolated all of the lines that seemed to him to have more than the required ten syllables and then, by comparing the actual instances, attempted to formulate a set of principles which could explain what Milton had been doing. In the main he forgot, as so many other prosodists have done, that what Milton had been doing was what the poets before him had done. Milton was operating in a well-known tradition. In his zeal to formulate principles, which he called "rules," Bridges turned to phonetics. Unfortunately, he was not a trained nor astute phonetician; he might have done better to adhere to descriptive principles that could have been tested by observation. Moreover, there is no reason to suspect that Milton, like Bridges, sought for complex phonetic explanations of any of his elisions. On the contrary, he constructed his devices on the models he found in Spenser and Shakespeare.

Bridges invented eight classifications of elision, and the phonetic principles that sometimes support them are highly original. In short, these classifications may be summarized in the following manner.

1. Vowel Elisions of Common Speech: By this Bridges refers to words containing contiguous vowels that were originally syllabic in common speech (e.g., *obedience*). Most of the words he discusses in this category end in *-ian* or *-ion*. He points out a few cases where the vowels are still syllabic in Milton (e.g., *consci-ence*, *Comus*, 212), but in most cases a disyllabic pronunciation has been replaced in British English by a monosyllabic

one. Further, he discusses in this category words that have not "established absolutely fixed values in English prosody."[6] These include hypermonosyllables, which he classifies as *-y* or *-w* glides. His examples of *-y* glides include *fire, desire, tire; -w* glides *power*. But it is never quite clear what Bridges meant by a glide, and sometimes he becomes very confusing.

2. The Poetic Elision of Vowels: About these Bridges says: "When two vowel sounds come together, then if the first of the two has a tail glide, there may be an elision, i.e. the sounds may be glided together so as to make a sound which can be reckoned as one syllable in the disyllabic verse . . . 'Diphthongs' are included and *-h* is often considered as no letter."[7] Again he speaks of two types of glides, but one difficulty with the category is that under it he considers too many examples of elision. For instance, common synaloepha, like *so oft* and *to ask*, are coupled with elisions concerning contiguous vowels in the same word, like *virtuous*.

3. Elision Through *-H:* This category refers to only one variety of synaloepha, the elision between two words, the first ending in a vowel, the second beginning with an aspirate. He also tries to explain this as a glide, though in fact no glide through *-h* is possible.

4. Poetic Elision of the Semivowels: Here Bridges discusses unaccented vowels in syllables closed by liquids and nasals, when they are followed by a syllable beginning with a vowel. He invents a special definition of the term *semivowel*, quite different from the common one. Again the category is too inclusive, containing *heaven* and *prison* (hypermonosyllables) alongside *wand'ring* and *glimmering* (elisions of the vowel preceding an intervocalic liquid).

5. The Rule of *-R:* Oddly, this "rule" covers exactly the same ground as the preceding one, and Bridges even cites *glimmering* again as an example. By this time his divisions have become hopelessly confused.

6. The Rule of *-L:* This is an extension of the "rule" of *-r*

6. Bridges, *Milton's Prosody*, 19.
7. *Ibid.*, 23.

15

to include the other liquid. Bridges lists examples both within and between words, but he does not take notice of cases where an *-able* termination precedes a word beginning with a vowel. This would be the place to include such matters if one intended to mention them at all.

7. The Rule of *-N:* He simply extends the former two "rules" to include the nasal *-n;* examples: *hardening* and *opening.*

8. Elision of Final Asyllabic *-N:* In this category Bridges discusses "the final syllabic semivowel *-n* as asyllabic."[8] Again *semivowel* has a special definition, but what he is discussing is clear, an elision of the final inflection; for example, *ris'n, eat'n.*

About a third of Bridges' book is devoted to Milton's treatment of syllables in elidible situations, and most of the discussion involves these "rules." Clearly such principles will permit a large number of exceptional cases, the discussion of which Bridges does not stint. Because of the highly original phonetic explanations Bridges conceived, later prosodists seem to have experienced great difficulty recognizing that the elisions Milton employed were really conventional devices for manipulating the number of syllables within the line, devices he inherited from a long poetic tradition.

In general Bridges' observations are very accurate, but his explanations are hopelessly confusing. His failure to recognize that he was dealing with a longstanding prosodic tradition caused him to seek overly subtle explanations, in an area where he was not fully competent, for observations that were excellent. Later writers, who do not understand Bridges' shortcomings, are sometimes tempted to invalidate the whole basis of his analysis. But that is unwarranted, for Bridges has made a significant contribution. He has shown that elisions are essentially metrical devices and that in English these are permissive in character. Not only that, but he has implied that in some cases elisions are fictive. That is to. say, no real cutting out of the syllable in question had to occur. Poets accepted certain situations as conventional. Nevertheless, metrical elision must have had its birth in linguistic change and in the growth of variant pronunciations.

8. *Ibid.,* 33.

16

However, one should not forget that the poets were familiar with the practice and not the explanation.

A final objection to the analysis in *Milton's Prosody* is that it was entirely qualitative. Bridges made no attempt to discover how much elision of one variety or another occurred in any particular selection and thus limited the usefulness of his study.

S. Ernest Sprott's Theory: Under normal circumstances Sprott's book might be eliminated from serious discussion,[9] not because it is inadequate and immature but because it rests on a fatal error in methodology. Sprott fails to cite anything but percentages; with no items listed it is impossible to check his accuracy. Accordingly, his readers cannot tell whether he was a careful observer or not. Certain of the percentages make us suspicious. For example, he cites two lists of feminine endings in *Comus, Paradise Lost, Paradise Regained*, and *Samson Agonistes*, both in percentages.[10] According to Sprott, the figures in the first column are comparable to those furnished by Professor Ants Oras in "Milton's Blank Verse and the Chronology of His Major Poems,"[11] except that Sprott's figures are percentages and Professor Oras expresses his in frequencies per 1000 lines. For Book I of *Paradise Lost* Sprott shows 1.1 per cent; Professor Oras cites a frequency of 12.5 per 1000 lines, indicating that his figure is based on 10 actual incidences. The difference here is not very significant; it would appear that Sprott failed to find one or two examples that Professor Oras discovered. For Book II, however, Sprott cites 0.4 per cent and Professor Oras, translating his figures to hundreds, 0.85 per cent. The difference is greater than 100 per cent, and from this point the two sets of figures are substantially different. My own observations agree with those of Professor Oras.

Besides accuracy, which cannot be checked because Sprott fails to supply sufficient evidence, another problem arises in this work because Sprott also fails to recognize that the devices of

9. That is, S. Ernest Sprott, *Milton's Art of Prosody*.
10. Sprott, 57.
11. Ants Oras, "Milton's Blank Verse and the Chronology of His Major Poems," in *SAMLA Studies in Milton*, ed. J. Max Patrick (Gainesville, Fla., 1953), 161.

metrical elision were traditional, and he proceeds from the categories Bridges invented. Like most of us, he finds these confusing and attempts to simplify them. He reduces elisions to contractions and synaloepha, though under these categories, broadly treated, he can discuss nearly everything observable. But difficulties arise when one tries to make comparisons. It is simply untenable to count *virtue hath* and *dissolute* (both metrically disyllabic) as examples of the same phenomenon and to intimate, however vaguely, that poets considered the two identical. It is very possible that poets never consciously thought of the types of elision discussed here, but because they constructed their elisions by analogy there is every indication that they considered, for example, *'twas, 'tis,* and *o're* one thing and *glimmering* another.

A further shortcoming of Sprott's study is his lack of interest in quantitative analysis of the treatment of syllables. Like Bridges, he seeks only to explain qualitatively what happened. Nevertheless, the study is not valueless if only because it reminds readers of certain principles that tend to be forgotten. For example, Sprott argues: "When once we have understood that elision is a technique of verse theory, that is, the process whereby Milton mentally removes a syllable which will not otherwise fit into his prosodical scheme, most of our difficulties over its acceptance will have vanished."[12] The alternative conclusion is to "forego the superior artistic unity conferred on a work by this restriction; one is at liberty to do so."[13] But as Sprott well knows and as his study reminds us, one is at liberty to do so only if he is willing to close his eyes to the overwhelming evidence of Milton's verse and the whole history of English syllabic prosody.

In one respect Sprott makes a suggestion that may contribute a new item to the theory of elision. He says that there may be cases "where the next line following may begin with a vowel with which the final syllable (under certain conditions) of the last word in the previous line may elide."[14] This is a very interesting

12. Sprott, 98.
13. *Ibid.*
14. *Ibid.,* 55.

18

idea, but unfortunately the four examples Sprott cites all concern lines where other elisions could explain the circumstances. For example, he calls our attention to a line ending in *luminarie*, followed by one beginning with *aloof*. But as the elision involved could as well be one over an intervocalic liquid, a fairly commonplace occurrence, there seems to be little need to seek a complex explanation.

HELEN DARBISHIRE'S EDITION: Finally we should examine the 1952 edition of *Paradise Lost* published by the Oxford Press. Previously Oxford had relied on the Beeching edition, first published in 1904, based on the first printed edition of the poem. One presumes that after nearly fifty years the publisher considered that edition outdated. Miss Darbishire's claim for the need of a new edition is based largely on spelling, the importance of which, she says, is "the main argument for a new text."[15] Anyone who examines the new edition will quickly see that it departs from many of the accepted principles of editing. It does so, however, on what might be a valid argument, if Miss Darbishire had actually discovered, as she believes, what Milton's spelling system was. There would then be good reason for a new edition to correct the many errors of various printers and, perhaps, different amanuenses. Miss Darbishire, however, fails, I believe, on two counts. First, she neglected to examine the evidence exhaustively. This is more important than it seems, for only a very comprehensive examination can reveal to what extent Milton, who apparently did use some sort of spelling system, was consistent. Second, Miss Darbishire at times, perhaps quite unintentionally, suppresses metrical evidence, though she must have employed some metrical criteria. How, for instance, can she be sure that *heav'n* (with an apostrophe) is monosyllabic without any metrical criteria at all? Indeed, *heav'n* (with apostrophe) is usually monosyllabic, but by assuming that the apostrophe in *heav'n* or *giv'n* indicates a cutting out of a vowel, Miss Darbishire works herself into an inconsistency, for she also assumes that the same mark before a syllabic *-n* or *-l* means just the op-

15. Helen Darbishire (ed.), *The Poetic Works of John Milton* (Oxford, 1952), I, ix.

posite. In my opinion the apostrophe in *op'n*, for example, is merely a spelling convention and not, as she argues, the sign of a syllabic vowel. To support her case, Miss Darbishire cites *forbidd'n*, but that is not very convincing evidence. It occurs three times with an elided final syllable in *Paradise Lost*, twice with the apostrophe and once without it.

There is already some doubt then about Miss Darbishire's first rule, that an apostrophe before *-n* or *-l* indicates a syllabic vowel. It is not difficult to find the evidence Miss Darbishire has used. In Book V, for instance, we find *burd'nd*, *hast'n*, and *startl'd* as disyllables; *forbidd'n*, *disheart'nd*, *assembl'd*, *forsak'n* as trisyllables. In Book VI there are more: *bustl'd*, *clov'n*, *mangl'd*, *heav'ns*, *hidd'n*, *settl'd*, *stumbl'd*, *hightn'd*, *hard'nd*, *disburd'nd*, *list'n*, all with an apostrophe where a syllabic vowel might be (these examples are listed in the order of their occurrence). In some books there are more examples. As Miss Darbishire understood, *-l'd* termination is syllabic in certain other spelling systems (particularly Ben Jonson's), but there the *-l* very often appears to be a syllabic *-l* anyhow, suggesting that the apostrophe indicates no more than that the vowel of the *-ed* inflection was cut out, perhaps in imitation of standard speech. The same may be true of Milton. Certainly the apostrophe in such words does not have to indicate a syllabic vowel at all, as Miss Darbishire believes. Probably in these cases there is no syllabic vowel, but rather we are confronted with a syllabic *-l*. If Milton had wished to indicate a syllabic vowel, there is no reason why he should not have written it rather than employ an apostrophe. However, in normal English, words ending in *-le* sometimes do have a syllabic vowel and other times merely a syllabic *-l*, depending to some extent on the speaker. Perhaps some of the poets, those who were particularly careful of their spelling, considered the possibility that a spelling like *tabled* could be mistaken by a reader (perhaps even for a trisyllable). In order to avoid ambiguity they might have inserted an apostrophe to indicate that the inflectional vowel was supposed to be silent (e.g., *tabl'd*). This seems to be the explanation for the 42 cases Miss Darbishire has in mind.

Some 79 other occurrences involve *-n* (alone—37; *-nd*—37; *-ns*—2; *-nst*—2; *-ning*—1). This is still not a great deal of evidence, but here I think Miss Darbishire is at least partly right. The poet does not seem to indicate with an apostrophe the presence of a syllabic nasal. That contention, however, would suggest that Milton was inconsistent about spelling phonetically, thus detracting from Miss Darbishire's central argument. One can partially agree with her, that Milton tried frequently to "indicate the precise sounds he requires for the reading of his lines: they are in fact a necessary part of his technique as a metrical artist."[16] Absolute consistency, however, was not part of that technique. Moreover, in these 79 instances it would have been just as easy for Milton to indicate a vowel sound by writing the letter which symbolizes it. I believe that an explanation for the apparent inconsistency we have discovered lies in the fact that in Milton's speech, in these cases, there may actually have been no vowel involved. He may have used a syllabic nasal, and, realizing this (however he might have verbalized it), felt it important to indicate that with an apostrophe.[17] On the other hand, the 79 instances could simply be misprints that eluded the proofreaders; it seems most unlikely that Milton had the whole 10,000 lines of the poem spelled back to him. In at least three instances he allowed a *th'* to stand where no elision of the vowel is required. In two other cases he allowed the spelling *e're* (VII.304 and VIII.273). If, as seems likely, he reserved this spelling for the contraction of *ever*, the first of these instances is an error, and the second may also be wrong. Milton frequently used *ere* (from OE *aer*) to mean "precedent in time." In the first book of *Paradise Lost* (line 150) there is an occurrence of the spelling with an apostrophe, unquestionably meaning *ever*. After that he seems to have thought the contraction

---

16. *Ibid.*, xviii.

17. Wyld, 403. Wyld also considers the possibility that Milton intended the apostrophe in these instances to indicate a syllabic nasal, but he rejects this theory on the grounds of inconsistency in Milton's practice. Wyld's observations are unquestionably correct; however, he does not take into account the frequency with which the apostrophe occurs where a syllabic nasal might have been intended.

of *ever* would be confusing (with the possible exception in Book VIII).

Miss Darbishire's second rule for the use of the apostrophe is that it indicates elision. Very often this is correct. She cites 24 instances of the spelling *giv'n* as a monosyllable (I find 25) in *Paradise Lost*, but she is ready to accept only two of the spelling *given* as monosyllabic. Presumably these are V.454 and IX.951. She halfway rejects an occurrence at XII.287:

And there/fore was / law giv*en* / them to / evince

In this line the *-en* in unstressed position is almost certainly not intended to be a metrical syllable, particularly in view of the following word. There is another instance in Book V where *given* precedes *him;* Miss Darbishire accepts this one as an instance of elision, though the word is fully spelled, but it is not possible to ascertain just what sort of elision she thought occurred. It is difficult to understand why she accepts some instances and rejects others.

Finally, Miss Darbishire often fails to recognize metrical elision at all. "*The earth* and *the air*," she says, "are the usual forms, representing two metrical syllables; *th'earth* representing one metrical syllable occurs a few times, *th'air* only twice."[18] She is right about *th'air;* however, *the aire* (without apostrophe) also occurs twice as an elision. *Th' earth* occurs more than a few times; I find ten and also *th' earths.* Moreover, *the earth* (without apostrophe) also occurs elided at least six times.

The entire case rests on such evidence. When Miss Darbishire fails to recognize the metrical elisions involved and when she sometimes neglects to cite all the pertinent facts, she damages her argument. Surely, there is some truth to the premise that Milton employed a spelling system, but that he was sufficiently consistent to warrant a new edition has not been proved. Accordingly, I have based this study on the H. C. Beeching text, which in turn was carefully based on the 1667 edition, though in fact there are not a great many differences between Beeching's edition and Miss Darbishire's that would affect these conclusions. In two

18. Darbishire, xxvii-xxviii.

cases I have accepted Miss Darbishire's reading in preference to Beeching's, both instances where she prints the 1674 text because a word has clearly been dropped in the printing of the earlier edition. Beeching, of course, cites these differences in a footnote.[19]

19. A strong practical consideration involved in the selection of the Beeching edition for a text has been the fact that many studies of Milton's prosody are based on that edition.

4. MILTON'S QUANTITATIVE USE OF ELISION

Tables 1 and 2 supply the figures for Milton's use of elision, the first showing the actual number of elisions involved and the second translating the figures into the frequency per 1000 lines. Table 2 indicates that Milton began *Paradise Lost* with a very heavy use of metrical devices, 391/1000 lines. That is a much higher frequency than we are accustomed to find in other poets and the highest to be found in Milton. This high frequency is accounted for primarily by Milton's extensive use of elision over contiguous vowels, synaloephae, and elision over liquids and nasals in Book I, though the first category is the most significant. There is no way of knowing why Milton composed in this fashion, which is really contrary to the practice of most poets. Usually the techniques of metrical elision develop and become more complex throughout a poet's career, which is substantially the same as saying that poets broadened the base of their techniques by adding gradually more and more elidible instances (though sometimes poets also discovered additional categories). But in *Paradise Lost* the opposite happens. Milton had thought his system through before he began the poem, and perhaps he was somewhat more attentive to his system in the first book, where doubtless he had to consider it consciously, than later after it became second nature to him.

As one might expect after examining Professor Oras' figures for the frequency of pauses of all varieties, or polysyllables, and run-on lines, there is a break in Milton's technique after the sixth book. This break would appear even sharper had the seventh book been of average length. But the seventh is the shortest book, and Milton has a tendency at times to crowd more elisions into the first half than the second. If Books VII and VIII are added together, then the break after Book VI is magnified. The frequency of elision for the two books (VII and VIII) together becomes 320/1000 lines, compared to 351/1000 lines for Books V and VI added together.

In the first six books, there is considerable elision in the initial book, the next two are about average, the fourth is relatively low, and the fifth and sixth are about average again. That pattern is almost repeated in the second half of the poem on a slightly lower scale. The initial book (that is, the seventh) is relatively high, the eighth about average for that half of the poem, the ninth (that is, the third book in the second half instead of the fourth, as in the first half) is low, and the last three are about average again.

The total frequency of Milton's elision by books in *Paradise Lost* supports Professor Hanford's contention that the poem may very likely have been interrupted in the middle of production. While this conclusion seems undoubtedly valid (there is a great deal of evidence to support it), analysis of the frequencies of the varieties of elision does not always point in that direction. In the most frequent category of elision, however, that over contiguous vowels, there is an apparent break in technique after the sixth book. The low spots that appear in the total frequency do not seem to be very significant for this variety of elision. Synaloephae are especially rare in Books IV, VI, VIII, IX, XI, and XII, and occur only in the final half of Book VIII. Less use of elision over liquids and nasals is made in Books VI and IX than otherwise in the respective halves of the poem, and significantly less use of hypermonosyllables is made in Books IX, X, XI, and to some degree in XII. The practice regarding hypermonosyllables may be partially explained in terms of the content of the poem, as the most frequent hypermonosyllable is the word *heav'n*. This situation suggests that the devices of elision are properly to be thought of as of a metrical nature; there is a point at which their use becomes almost unconscious, though by and large Milton seems to have planned rather carefully whether he employs devices with more or less frequency in one or another portion of the poem.

25

5. MILTON'S QUALITATIVE USE OF ELISION

HYPERMONOSYLLABLES: There is no significant change in Milton's use of these devices throughout the poem. After *heav'n, power(s)* is the most frequent hypermonosyllable. In fact one finds just about the same hypermonosyllables in every book with one exception; in Books IX, X, and XI there are one or two instances of *evil* and *devil* elided. The former is used rather consistently throughout the poem as a disyllable; however, in a few cases Milton intended it to be a monosyllable. Of course there is always the possibility that in those cases he meant to compose a line with a real extrametrical syllable, but he is so entirely consistent about denying such lines throughout the poem that the possibility should be discounted. *Devil* does not occur very often, and we cannot say that he employed it more one way than another. After Book IX Milton increased his list of hypermonosyllables slightly. There may in fact be a few more occurrences than appear in the Appendix, for I have tabulated three instances of *devilish* with elisions over the liquid *-l*. Milton may have considered these also to be hypermonosyllables, or at least analagous to them.

One should certainly first point to *heav'n* as an example of this category:

Th' Apoc/alyps, / heard cry / in *Heav'n* / aloud (IV.2)

Heav'n occurs thirty times written as an elided form in this book (Book IV), and twice it occurs elided but fully spelled:

A *Heaven* / on Earth: / for bliss/ful Par/adise (IV.208)

Miss Darbishire suggests that line 208 was a mistake on the part of either the amanuensis or the printer, but I cannot agree. There is no reason why we should expect Milton to have been entirely consistent, though indeed he was perhaps more so than any English poet before him. But the seventeenth century mind simply did not place our values on consistency.

This word also appears as a disyllable:

From my / prevail/ing arme, / though *Heav/ens* King
(IV.973)

That is what we should expect of an elision, though it is perhaps remarkable how seldom Milton used this particular word disyllabically.

ELISIONS OVER LIQUIDS AND NASALS: Except that the evidence would be very slight in each, this category might be divided into three subcategories: elisions over the liquid *-r*, over the liquid *-l*, and over the nasal *-n*. About 80 per cent of the elisions are over the liquid *-r*, and there is very slight qualitative difference in Milton's technique among the books of *Paradise Lost*. Most of these elisions concern the cutting out of a vowel, usually a neutral one, preceding an *-r* within a word, usually an *-r* before a suffix of one sort or another. Examples may be found in words like *answering*, and *wondring* (usually spelled without an *-e*), *temperance, reverence*, and *amorous*. There are a few cases where Milton seems to have extended the principle to operate between words, possibly by analogy with synaloepha. *Pillar of* seemed highly fictive to Bridges, but another example, *river of*, makes the former elision more plausible.

The same words occur over and over again in the lists for each book, but gradually Milton adds new examples. Most of these elisions are still familiar to us in either pronunciation. Milton sometimes indicates the elided pronunciation by his spelling and sometimes does not. With some words he tends to indicate elision with considerable consistency of spelling; with others he almost never spells phonetically. *Glistering* always has an *-e* before the *-r*, but *glist'ning* substitutes an apostrophe before the *-n*. Both are disyllables. *Wandring*, which occurs fairly frequently, is always spelled without an *-e*, except once; it is never trisyllabic.[1] *General* is always spelled with the *-e* before the *-r*

---

1. There is some doubt about *wandering* which appears consistently in the Renaissance as a disyllable, but never, to my recollection, as a trisyllable. Perhaps it was not an intentional elision at all; Bridges, however, accepted it and

and is invariably disyllabic, but that Milton was aware of its potentialities seems indicated by his treatment of *several*, which is also almost invariably disyllabic but on at least one occasion is spelled *sev'ral*. In other poets *general* was occasionally trisyllabic.

Words like *sovran* are much more difficult to classify, because this is a special Miltonic spelling for *sovereign*, according to the *Oxford English Dictionary*. Other writers usually spelled the word trisyllabically, though elision frequently took place. The occurrence of the spelling *sov'ranty* (with apostrophe) on one occasion clearly suggests that Milton thought of the word as an example of a device of poetic elision.

The word most commonly elided in this category is *spirit(s)* (or *spiritual*—often a disyllable). In this case there is no way of making certain which vowel is being elided because it is not possible to determine how Milton pronounced the monosyllabic form. But Bridges had a theory about this matter which seems quite logical; the first vowel, he argued, cannot have been elided because it is stressed. But if the second vowel is elided, Bridges claims, the word becomes an exception to Milton's practice.[2] This may or may not be a valid contention. His second argument, it seems to me, is stronger, that if the initial vowel were the one elided we should end up with *sprite*. He believes that if Milton had wanted *sprite* he would have written it. There remains the possibility of an elision parallel to that found in Italian (*spir'to:* Dante, *Inferno*, V.139). This argument is very persuasive without being entirely convincing, because Milton consistently elides the vowel preceding *-r*. It is also possible, however, that Milton thought of *spirit* more as a hypermonosyllable than an elision in this category.

The following lines are typical examples of elision in this category:

She all / night long / her am/*oro*us des/cant sung (IV.603)

---

used it as an example, and it would seem unwarranted therefore to exclude it altogether. For further discussion of this phonetic phenomenon, but not this particular word, see Wyld, 407.

2. Bridges, *Milton's Prosody*, 34.

Glistring / with dew; / fragant / the fer/til earth (IV.645)
And from / thir Iv/*orie* Port / the Cher/ubim (IV.778)
Think not, / revolt/ed Sp*irit*, / thy shape / the same (IV.835)

And for the other side of the matter (that is, no elision):

And sweet / reluc/tant am/*orous* / delay (IV.311)
Add Ver/tue, Pat/ience, Temp/*erance*, / add Love
(XII.583)
Though not / but by / the Sp*ir*/*it* un/derstood (XII.514)

Elisions over the liquid -*l* are far less frequent and somewhat
more difficult to explain. Words like *popular, populous, credulous, ridiculous,* and *jav'lin* seem to belong to this category,
though it is hard to believe that the entire vowel sound preceding the liquid was cut out, except in a few words like *jav'lin.*
A handful of other words, like *devillish* and *violate,* are questionable examples, but there is little doubt Milton thought of
them as elidible forms of some sort. Most interesting here is the
fact that Milton permits elision between words, particularly
those ending in -*le* (where the sound is [əl] or [l̩]). There are
a few clear-cut instances, like *people and, temple enshrined,* but
most cases are more complex because they involve the elision of
the suffix -*able* or, sometimes, -*ible.* For example, *invisible else,
innumerable or, imaginable as, immeasurable abyss* occur. Cases
of this type are difficult to classify because we do not know how
Milton accented the suffix. To be sure, the accent usually falls
on the -*a* in -*able,* particularly in compounds, but there are still
a good many cases where it does not.[3] Usually these lines are
treated as follows:

O mis/era/ble Man/kind, to / what fall (XI.497)

However, not infrequently Milton will do the opposite:

Not un/agree/able, / to found / a path (X.256)
Howev/er in/support/able, / be all (X.134)

The difficulty in placing such cases arises when the suffix fol-

3. On this point Bridges' observations are not very reliable.

lows a liquid or a nasal, or even perhaps a sibilant, for then it is not possible to be certain that Milton did not intend a somewhat unusual elision over a liquid or nasal rather than the elision between words. On the other hand, there is no reason to believe he would hesitate to use the elision between words; an analogy with the more common synaloepha certainly did not escape his attention, and of course elisions like *purple and* are undeniable.

Elisions over intervocalic nasals operate just as do those over liquids. Milton is very fond of *cov'nant, count'nance,* and *op'ning,* but there are also a good many in which he does not usually indicate the elision with an apostrophe; for example, *original, bituminous, reasoning,* and *ravenous.* One also finds *rav'nous* and on at least one occasion in Book XI the full spelling of *covenant* (still a disyllable), a word where he almost always uses the apostrophe. It seems Milton permitted elision between words in this category also; he uses such expressions as *garden and,* and *reason and,* though he also sometimes writes *gard'n of* or *eat'n and.* The apostrophe is troublesome to explain because an apostrophe before a final -*n* is sometimes the sign of a non-syllabic final nasal, regardless of whether it precedes a word beginning with a vowel or not. But this distinction is probably too fine. It is doubtful Milton was so subtle, and besides it makes little difference in our tabulations because the number of instances is so small.

SYNALOEPHAE: (Renaissance rhetoricians sometimes prefer to speak of *crasis.*) Milton's synaloephae are of two general varieties: (1) those that concern the dropping of a vowel from a short monosyllable, usually the article, before a word beginning with a vowel, and (2) those that concern the dropping of a final syllable from a disyllable or longer word under exactly the same conditions. He also elides before an aspirate, but only infrequently; on a very few occasions he may elide before a semivowel. He does use *t' whom* twice in Book II and once each in Books VI and XI; these are remarkable examples because they are also the only instances in which he indicates an elision of the preposition with an apostrophe. On 33 other occasions *to* is metrically elided before a vowel without there being any indica-

tion in the spelling.[4] These cases are about evenly divided between the first and second halves of the poem (14 in the first
half, 19 in the second). On the other hand, Milton prefers to
use *th'* when he wishes to indicate an elision. This device occurs 273 times in the poem (166 in the first half, 107 in the second). The difference between halves of the poem, in this
respect, does not seem very significant, for Milton does not turn
very strongly in the second half to *the* in place of *th'*. He employs *the* 34 times in the poem (15 times in the first half, 19
in the second). Miss Darbishire leaves her readers with the im-
pression that *the* in an elidible situation is actually a mistake,
but there is no reason for believing that. She suppresses, or perhaps was unaware of, the fact that *the* occurs 34 times in elidible
situations. While this is not an extremely large number of occurrences, it is still more evidence than she often relies on—and
it is too many instances to be lightly explained away as misprints.

There are really no appreciable differences, then, between the
two halves of *Paradise Lost* with regard to synaloepha. In the
first half approximately 65 per cent of the synaloephae depend
on elision of the article or the preposition *to;* in the second half
the figure is 61 per cent. One peculiarity with regard to this
category has already been noted of Book VIII; there Milton
makes but slight use of synaloephae, and almost all of these instances are found in the second half of the book. There is no
ready explanation for this phenomenon other than that he simply
felt like making a change in his technique at this point. It is possible, however, to suggest a possible reason from an examination
of the contents of the book, for Book VIII is largely given over,
particularly at the beginning, to speeches made by Adam. The
careful reader may note that throughout the poem Adam is
somewhat parsimonious about the use of metrical elision, though
he certainly does not refrain from it with any great consistency.
Perhaps Milton felt that Adam, whose role is always a very
serious one, should speak very deliberately, or even very slowly

4. Miss Darbishire has neglected this evidence, which seems to detract from
her argument. Can she possibly be reading 33 instances where *to* precedes a
vowel in elidible situations as extrametricals? She does not remove the -*o* and
substitute an apostrophe in her text.

31

in keeping with his primitive, simple nature, but of course the lack of elision in his speeches may be mere fortuitous circumstance. There are some slight indications that Milton did occasionally employ metrical elisions to emphasize the content of particular passages. He did not, however, do so very often. Nor was he consistent; at one point God may speak with many elisions, at another with very few. But even a faint suggestion of such a use of these metrical devices represents a great step forward in metrical technique. Previously no poet, except perhaps Shakespeare, appears to have thought of using such devices to emphasize action or delineate character.[5]

Examples of synaloepha are too common to require much attention. The first two of the following deal with the article:

In pres/ence of / th' *A*lmight/ie Fath/er, pleas'd (VII.11)
When such / was heard / declar'd / the *A*lmight/ie's will
(VII.181)
And vit/al ver/*tue* *i*nfus'd, / and vit/al warmth (VII.236)
Of Rain/bows and / Starr*ie* *E*yes. / The Wat/ers thus
(VII.447)

It may be noted that as Milton progressed he grew more daring with synaloepha, though the process begins quite early in the poem. In Book III we find *justly accuse, timely interposes,* and *easie ascent* in addition to the more commonplace examples, *many a, shadow of,* and *mercy and.* By the time he reaches Book X, such combinations occur as *sorrow abandoned, sorrow infeignd, adversarie his, dutie erewhile, fully avenged, they assayd.*

ELISION OVER CONTIGUOUS VOWELS: (Sometimes called synizesis in Renaissance rhetorics.) This is the variety of elision Milton employs most extensively. There are 1,024 examples (plus or minus a few of doubtful validity) in *Paradise Lost.* As noted, there is a distinct break in the category after the sixth

5. In a forthcoming study, *The Osier Cage* (University of Kentucky Press) I have attempted to show that Shakespeare uses rhetorical devices in a similar manner, and, it is worth remembering, rhetorical and metrical devices were often in the sixteenth and seventeenth centuries considered as part of the same technique.

book. The frequency is 111 per 1000 lines in the first half of the poem, 82 per 1000 lines in the second (that is, 601 actual elisions of the variety in the first half, 5,426 lines, and 423 in the second half, 5,132 lines).

By far the majority of elisions over contiguous vowels occur in terminal syllables where a phonetic combination that approximates [ɪ], as in *celestial, ethereal, immediate, various, illustrious,* is reduced to what may have approximated [jə]. A good many other combinations may be cited, but their frequencies are dwarfed by the number of times the one above appears. There is no way of ascertaining exactly how these and similar terminations sounded in Milton's speech. In present American speech, for example, the separate vowels in terminations of this nature are sometimes clearly distinguishable; at other times, depending on the word involved and the individual speaker, they are not. For example, *celestial* is a word with four distinct syllables in the speech of many Americans (a dialect often supposed to be closer to seventeenth century English than present Received Standard British English). In British English, however, this word often has only three syllables; the *-ial* termination has undergone synizesis; elision has occurred. But with Milton, we should remember, no real diphthongization was necessary for an elision to be understood. His practice was a matter of metrical convention. It seems, then, that the two final syllables, reduced to one in the verse, of words such as *Proteus* or *Uriel* are really "fictional diphthongizations."[6] There is no evidence that Milton said [protiəs], though that pronunciation is now current. In many cases it does not seem possible for Milton to have concealed the individual vowel qualities entirely without serious distortion.

One need not search far for examples of this variety of elision; there is one in the first line of the poem:

Of Man's First Disobed*i*ence, and the Fruit

---

6. *Uriel* may have had a disyllabic pronunciation, not unlike rural American (dænəl) for *Daniel* (unquestionably a survival from earlier British). Also *McDannell* is a Scot variant for *McDaniel*. Hence *Uriel* as a disyllable may have been more than a literary elision.

Certain words of this sort occur over and over again in their elided forms. Among his favorites are *being, hideous, glorious*. But Milton was also quite capable of using the expanded forms of these words. For example, the *-iel* termination is fully sylla-bized three times in Book IV in *Ithuriel* (4 metrical syllables), twice in *Gabriel* (3 metrical syllables). The last also occurs fairly frequently as a disyllable. Moreover, in Book IV he also uses *su-per-flu-ous* (usually a trisyllable), *am-i-a-blie*, and *in-flu-ence*. To these might be added a class of proper names, usually those of remote connotation, which generally he fully syllabizes, refraining from elision unless their pronunciation was fairly well known; for example, *Astrea* (3 metrical syllables), *Nyseian* (3 metrical syllables).[7] In Book V *pi-ous, Tob-i-as, hi-er-arch, eth-er-e-al, Raph-a-el, di-a-mond, vi-o-lence* all oc-cur, words that are also frequently found elided. The list could be extended, but these examples are enough to make it clear that, in this respect, Milton is dealing with a well-formulated practice of metrical elision.

NON-SYLLABIC *-EST* INFLECTION: At this juncture it seems desirable to depart from the procedure previously outlined to discuss verbal inflections. (Those few cases of *-est* as the sign of the superlative that have entered into these tabulations are properly dealt with under the category of elision over contigu-ous vowels.) For purposes of consistency all elided *-est* verbal inflections are considered here, even those which might have been included as elisions over contiguous vowels, the two most prominent examples being *seest* and *maist*. These elisions occur slightly more often in the last half of the poem than in the first; there are 133 in the last half and 108 in the first. But there is a question whether Milton intended all of them to be elisions or perhaps thought of some of them as normal pronunciations. He employs an apostrophe frequently but only with certain words. Words like *canst, maist* (or *mayst*), *seest, shouldst, knowst* occur almost without exception without an apostrophe;

---

7. He usually avoids eliding proper nouns of classical origin, unless they are fairly common names, with respect for all varieties of elision. For example *Hesperus* is a trisyllable, though it might readily undergo elision over *-r*.

QUALITATIVE USE

words like *gav'st, draw'st, took'st, fli'st, hear'st* generally have
one, indicating that a cutting out of the inflectional vowel was
certainly intentional and that elision took place. It is very puz-
zling for us to observe that while *shouldst* usually has no apostrophe, *would'st* generally has; *could'st,* which does not occur
very often, is found both ways. As it is not possible to ascertain beyond reasonable doubt what Milton intended, it has
seemed discreet to include nearly all verbs ending in *-st* in this
category, excepting only a very few, such as *hast,* which is
not an *-est* form anyhow. *Did-est* and *can-est* are of course very
farfetched (these spellings never occur in Milton), but it has
been necessary to include their syncopated forms in the tabulations to attain consistency. Besides, we must be careful of our
impressions of these matters; *went-est,* for instance, actually
occurs.

NON-SYLLABIC FINAL NASALS: These are largely confined to
three words: *giv'n, fall'n, driv'n;* a few others, such as *chos'n,*
ris'n, unshak'n do occur though very infrequently. There are
slightly fewer elisions of this nature in the second half of the
poem than in the first (43 instances compared to 46 in the first
half). Sometimes Milton indicates these elisions with an apostrophe, sometimes not; alongside of *giv'n* there is *given;* we also
find *falln, risen, forbidden, prison, drivn,* and possibly *reason.*

CONTRACTIONS: Almost 66 per cent of the common speech
contractions in *Paradise Lost,* used for poetic purposes as if they
were elisions, concern the single item *o're* for *over.* In 34 of
these instances the word stands by itself; in 12 cases it is part of a
compound. Usually the apostrophe occurs, indicating the cutting out of a vowel and hence a syllable, but in six cases the
apostrophe is omitted. The omission of the apostrophe need not
concern the reader, for it is clear from the context that it is the
contraction Milton intends and not the homonym; however, it is
of interest to note that once again Milton is not consistent.

It would seem that *e're* is, in a few instances, a contraction of
ever. In Book I, line 150, it is; there it is spelled with an apostrophe. In other cases where it is spelled without an apostrophe the
meaning seems to be "previous in time," suggesting that Milton

35

intended the different word *ere* (from OE *aer*). Of the two other instances in the poem with an apostrophe, Miss Darbishire corrects one (VII.304) and allows the other (VIII.273) to stand. She might also have found reasons for correcting the occurrence in Book VIII. (Accordingly, only the first of these contractions is included in this tabulation.)

This category must perforce serve as something of a catchall. Strictly speaking it does not seem proper to consider aphetic forms as contractions, but to make a further division of such a small amount of evidence hardly seems worthwhile. We may note the aphetic forms *gan* and *twixt*, both common in poetic diction, *scape*, and the form *sdeignd* for *disdained*.[8] Along with these are at least two instances of the form *submiss* for *submission*. These devices are confined almost entirely to the first half of the poem; there are only 17 contractions in the final half of the poem, six of them *o're*. About halfway through the poem Milton virtually abandoned the device.

8. The word *sdeignd* was surely borrowed from Spenser.

6. EXCEPTIONS TO THE PRINCIPLES OF ELISION

A few lines appear to be exceptions to the principles of metrical elision, or at least exceptions to Milton's usual practice in *Paradise Lost*. These are:

1. In bill/ows, leave / i' th' midst / a hor/rid Vale (I.224)
2. Creat/ed evil, / for e/vil on/ly good (II.623)
3. Som Cap/ital Cit/y, or less / then if / this frame (II.924)
4. Listens delighted. Eevning approachd (V.627)
5. For hee / who tempts, / though in vain, / at least / asperses (IX.296)
6. Both Good / and Evil, / Good lost, / and E/vil got (IX.1072)
7. Because / thou hast heark/'nd to / the voice / of thy wife (X.198)
8. With me; how can they acquitted stand (X.827)
9. Perhaps / thy Cap/ital Seate, / from whence / had spred (XI.343)
10. Ith' midst / an Al/tar as / the Land-/mark stood (XI.432)
11. Promisd / to Ab/raham and / his Seed: / the rest (XII.260)
12. From Ab/raham, Son / of Is/aac, and / from him (XII.268)
13. Just Ab/raham and / his Seed: / now first / I finde (XII.273)
14. Foretold / to Ab/raham, as / in whom / shall trust (XII.328)
15. Needs must / the Ser/pent now / his cap/ital bruise (XII.383)
16. Not one/ly to / the Sons / of Ab/rahams Loines (XII.447)

All of these lines, with the exceptions of 4 and 8, are the same

37

in Miss Darbishire's edition. In both of these exceptions she adopts the reading of the 1674 edition, which is undoubtedly correct. In line 4 the 1667 edition somehow omitted the word *now* before *approached*, and in line 8 the word *then* was left out before acquitted. Both lines are then regular decasyllables.

In lines 1 and 10, as far apart as Books I and XI, one is faced with what in Milton's system would seem an impossible elision indicated by the apostrophe after the article. The apostrophe after the -*i* in line 1 does not matter because so long as the vowel quality remains so does the syllabic value. There is really no way to rationalize these extrametricals; perhaps they are the fault of the amanuensis, who in reading the lines back to Milton somehow slurred over the article so that the poet failed to recognize that it was there. The lines would be just as sensible if the article, *th'*, were omitted.[1]

Lines 2 and 6 are exceptional because of the double occurrence in each of the word *evil*, first as a hypermonosyllable and then its more customary disyllabic form. As *evil* could be monosyllabic, the lines may be scanned as regular after the operation of elision, but the trick of using both forms in the same line is very unusual (though it is found in Chaucer). It is not hard to establish that *evil* had a monosyllabic form; Kökeritz, for example, calls attention to "*evil* [as a] monosyllable in *Cy*[*mbeline*] 1.1.72, 5.5.60, *M*[*acbeth*] 4.3.57, *MM* [*Measure for Measure*] 1.2.134. . . ."[2] If the word is monosyllabic in Shakespeare, there is no reason why it should not be in Milton.[3]

1. According to the *OED* a use without the article would be rare but by no means impossible. Spenser used "in middest" more than once, and an occurrence of "in midst" is recorded as early as 1617. On the other hand, the *ith'* construction does occur elsewhere in Milton, in the 1st Psalm (1653) in the line, "In counsel of the wicked, and ith' way." There, however, there is no question of an extrametrical syllable because the vowel of the article, which is indicated as elided, precedes a semivowel. It seems possible that the *ith'* construction may have been a special archaism that Milton occasionally employed and that it found its way into *Paradise Lost* as an exception, without his realizing that it constituted a departure from principle. Nevertheless the possibility that the construction was intentional seems to me more likely.

2. Helge Kökeritz, *Shakespeare's Pronunciation* (New Haven, 1953), 204.

3. Bridges points out that Milton also writes "knowledge of good and *ill*" for *evil* (*Milton's Prosody*, 32). But Kökeritz does not recognize the possibility that in Shakespeare *ill* may have been felt to be a different form from *evil*.

38

Lines 3, 9, and 15 appear to have a light extrametrical syllable depending on the word *capital*. None of the general principles of elision that we observe in Milton work here. But in his own speech Milton may have used a disyllabic pronunciation of the word; there is no trisyllabic occurrence in the poem. Milton was usually careful, if not consistent, about indicating his pronunciation, but if he commonly said something like [kæptḷ], the matter might have slipped his attention. That pronunciation is occasionally heard even today in British English. At any rate these few doubtful instances cannot be taken as evidence that Milton permitted extrametrical syllables.

Line 5 is exceptional because it contains a very odd elision, *though in*, but phonetically it works satisfactorily.

Line 7 will present no great difficulties to the attentive student, but it may puzzle the novice because it is barely possible to scan it as a hexameter. In the second foot there is an unfamiliar elision between *thou* and *hast*, though by no means an impossible one, and in the final foot an elision depends on what is rare in Milton, synaloepha across a semivowel.

Remaining to be explained are lines 11, 12, 13, 14, and 16, all of which appear to have an extrametrical because of the name *Abraham*. One might assume that Milton intended the pronunciation of the formal variant, *Abram*, in these instances, were it not for the biblical difficulties in which that might involve him. Of all poets Milton would have been most careful of such matters. But there is another possibility, that the name was pronounced in some way in which the *-h* was silent, not unlike the present British pronunciation of *Wilbraham* [wɪlbrɪəm]. In that case an elision between contiguous vowels would account for the apparent extrametrical syllable.[4]

4. C. W. Bardsley in the *Dictionary of English and Welsh Surnames* (London, 1901) records the spelling *Abraam* under *Abraham* in Middle English. Eilert Ekwall in the *Concise Oxford Dictionary of English Place Names* records a spelling of *Walsham* from which the *-h* has been lost, *Walessam*. This is somewhat parallel to the modern pronunciation of *Birmingham* (in England) from which *-h* has been dropped. But that is not quite the same thing that happened in *Abraham* because *-ham* in place names comes from an Old English form of the word *home*. However such phenomena suggest that this hypothetical explanation of Milton's elision may not be so farfetched after all.

7. DEGREE OF SYLLABIC REGULARITY IN *PARADISE LOST*

The amount of metrical elision in each book of *Paradise Lost* may quickly be read from Table 2. But these figures do not entirely indicate what the degree of syllabic regularity is. In the first place, many lines have multiple elisions in them, sometimes, it would seem, for purposes of emphasizing the content of this or that particular line. For example:

Gambold before them, th'unwieldy Elephant (IV.345)
Gabriel, thou hadst in Heav'n th'esteem of wise (IV.886)
Wallowing unweildie, enormous in thir Gate (VII.411)

In the first and last of these lines the elisions seem to be calculated to enhance the feeling of ponderousness, while in the second line, which begins a speech by Satan to an angel, the elisions seem to emphasize the snarling, defiant mood of the archfiend.

Milton averages an elision about every four lines, but in reality there are sometimes long passages with no elisions at all followed by other passages in which the elisions are crowded on top of each other. But lines with elision do not make the poem irregular in terms of Milton's system, although their effect is not exactly the same as that of regular decasyllables. There are, then, as we have seen, only 16 lines in the whole poem about which there is any doubt concerning their decasyllabic intention. All of these are capable of explanation, some perhaps as exceptional cases. If, however, we choose to disregard all of these explanations, which would seem unwarranted, the poem still contains more than 99 per cent regular decasyllables, once the elisions are understood.

8. FEMININE ENDINGS AND SYLLABIZED -*ED* ENDINGS

Strictly speaking neither of these devices concerns metrical elision, but as they concern the number of syllables in the line it is desirable to mention both. Syllabized -*ed*'s occur in both halves of *Paradise Lost*, though there are fewer in the second half than in the first. Feminine endings are very infrequent in the first half of the poem and only slightly more common in the second half, but their quality changes in the second half. There they are unmistakable feminine endings; whereas, in the first half of the poem a large number of them could be taken for elision in end-line position. I have nothing further to add on these subjects, both of which have received extensive treatment in Professor Oras' "Milton's Blank Verse and the Chronology of His Major Poems."[1]

1. *SAMLA Studies in Milton.*

9. ELISIONS IN
PARADISE REGAINED

Doubtless, Milton's practice reached its apex in *Paradise Lost*, and that is the ideal place, as Bridges and the others have agreed, to study his technique. There we find elisions employed with the greatest frequency in his works, and we also have available for investigation fine editions that were almost certainly supervised through the press. *Paradise Regained*, however, is nearly as interesting, though in a different way. There we find (see Table 3) that on the whole the quantity of elision used in the poem compares closely with that in the last six books of *Paradise Lost:* I have tabulated 597 elisions in the 2,070 lines; that is, a frequency of 288 per 1000 lines. That is what we should expect considering the chronology of the poem.

But bare statistics can be misleading. Actually, it is Books I and IV of *Paradise Regained* that compare closely with the last six books of the longer poem. Books II and III balance each other with frequencies of 249 and 350 elisions per 1000 lines, respectively. Book III, with a rate of 350 elisions per 1000 lines, compares very closely with Books III, V, or VI of *Paradise Lost*. Indeed the high incidence of elision in Book III suggests that Milton may have been reworking earlier material in the preparation of that book, though an examination of other metrical devices and of the elisions themselves indicates that he was certainly not simply adapting something he had done about the time he wrote the first half of *Paradise Lost*. Book III of *Paradise Regained*, for instance, contains a few very heavy feminine endings that would never have been permitted in the longer poem (e.g., *them*, III.440).

Book II is also very interesting because there the total frequency of elision, 249 per 1000 lines, compares almost exactly with that in *Samson Agonistes*, his last great poetic work. (In *Samson* there are 245 per 1000 lines.) There is some reason, then, to suspect that Book II may have been the latest of the four books of *Paradise Regained* to be written, but another explanation also suggests itself. It seems possible that when Milton wrote Book II he permitted his attention to stray from the question of elision, even though he was usually very careful about such matters. I do not think we can charge Milton with carelessness, but it is always possible that something else demanded his attention at the time. A poet, after all, cannot keep everything in mind at once, not even Milton. I suggest that is what happened. There are some reasons to believe that in Book II Milton was beginning to experiment with elision not only as a metrical device, calculated primarily for euphonic variation, but was beginning to consider the possibilities of defining character in these terms. For example, simple characters, as the Virgin Mary, speak with very little elision. Satan and Christ are the great exponents of the device. In fact at places in Book II Satan and Christ seem to be engaged in a metrical duel, much more subtle but not unlike the rhetorical battles of repartee that Shakespeare loved so well.[1] Unfortunately, Book II is not the only place where Milton appears to be thinking of elisions as functional devices. There were some hints of this technique in *Paradise Lost*; now the technique of Book II seems to be carried over into Book III (indicating how careful we should be about jumping to conclusions about the chronology of the books on statistical evidence).

Notice the following lines, which turn on the key word *glory:*

> Think not so slight of glory; therein least,
> Resembling thy great Father: he seeks glory,
> And for his glory all things made, all things
> Orders and governs, nor content in Heaven
> By all his Angels glorifi'd, requires
> Glory from men, from all men good or bad,
>   (III.109-14)

In this passage Satan is speaking of the glory of God. There is nothing unusual about his use of the word except the repetition, which becomes rather burdensome, but it seems clear that Satan

1. I am presently engaged in a more extensive study of these matters in *Paradise Regained*.

43

is permitting the idea of God's glory, and his own reiteration of the word, to arouse his temper. In each instance thus far, *glory* is used separately; that is, it is not involved in a metrical elision, though in line 110 it provides a feminine ending. But now Satan realizes that the word itself is making him angry, and allowing his pride to gather, he shows off his metrical gift to Jesus:

> Glory *he* / requires,/and glor/y he / receives (III.117)

Here he indulges in a rather unusual synaloepha before an aspirate, pointing it out to us by using the word over again in the same line unelided. And he stresses his skill a little later, repeating the same device:

> From us his foes pronounc't / glory *he* / exacts (III.120)

It is the last line of a speech filled with sophistry wherein he attempts to persuade Jesus that God is seeking his own glory. He is treating Jesus rather contemptuously and showing off his rhetorical ability at the same time.

This display does not go unnoticed. In the speech in which Jesus answers Satan, we find the very unusual line:

> But why should man / seek glor/y? *who* of / his own
> (III.134)

Here Milton permits Jesus to use an even rarer sort of synaloepha, as if to put Satan in his place by implying that his great poetic ability is not enough to help him now that he has fallen. And just so Satan, and the reader, will not miss the point, Jesus ends the speech:

> That who advance his glory, not thir own,
> Them he himself to glory will advance. (III.143-44)

Doubtless, there are several other such passages in *Paradise Regained* where Milton experiments with a functional use of elision.

Examination of the statistics for the particular categories of elision in the poem may not be very significant because the number of instances is small; the books are considerably shorter than those in *Paradise Lost*. The high incidence of hypermonosyllables in the first book seems to have been deliberately balanced by a reduction of elisions over liquids and nasals. As one might expect, the word *heaven* accounts for most of the occurrences. One other point is worth noting about the incidence of elision over contiguous vowels. In *Paradise Regained* Milton actually seems to be trying to depress this usage. There are a great many proper names in the poem ending in *-ia*, *-ian*, and very often Milton affords them their full complement of syllables. A few, such as *Parthian*, he almost always elides, and that may indeed represent his own pronunciation.

10. ELISIONS IN *COMUS*
AND *SAMSON AGONISTES*

This study would not be complete without presenting the evidence with respect to Milton's first and last lengthy poems. Neither, of course, is composed entirely of decasyllables. The tabulations that follow (Table 4) are based on the decasyllabic lines; that is, for *Comus* lines 1-92, 145-299, and 244-858 (omitting seven broken lines that fall in the decasyllabic passages), a total of 785 lines. For *Samson* 479 chorus lines have been omitted and lines 606-51, a lyrical speech by Samson, making a total of 1,233 lines used. (The frequencies in Table 4 are based on these figures.)

It should be immediately clear that Milton had not fully developed his system of elision when he wrote *Comus*. Quantitatively he used only 182 elisions per 1000 lines, and qualitatively he was freer in this poem, sticking less rigidly to the categories he later adopted, than elsewhere. When he wrote *Comus*, he seems to have been well acquainted with the tradition of metrical elision, but he was not quite at home with the practices.

In *Samson* he uses these devices with less frequency than he did in *Paradise Lost* or *Paradise Regained*, except for the second book of the latter poem. Perhaps his interest was, to some extent, tapering off, but there is another ready explanation. Elisions are largely devices used to secure variation in the line, but in *Samson* the need to secure variation is not so great as in the epic poems because the decasyllabic passages are broken by the choruses. Furthermore, in *Samson* Milton made great use of feminine endings in the decasyllabic portions, a practice which also tends to alleviate tediousness in the verse.

The reader is invited to compare the frequencies per 1000 lines for each category of elision to ascertain how Milton's practice developed throughout his career.

11. SUMMARY OF
MILTON'S PRACTICE

It is abundantly clear that Milton employed the traditional system of metrical elision that had been the heritage of English poets since Chaucer. To this system he added no new categories. He did, however, show great virtuosity in his treatment of each variety of elision. In fact the list of words, and combinations of words, that Milton permitted to elide is greater than that of any other poet in the language, and on this circumstance his claim to perfecting the entire technique of handling these devices must largely rest.

Also, the tables indicate that elision was a technique that Milton had to learn as a practicing poet. In *Comus* he used it with noticeable lack of sureness; his total use of these devices in that poem amounts to only 182 elisions per 1000 lines. With respect to the amount of use made of elision, Milton reached his peak in the first half of *Paradise Lost*, particularly in the first book. Thereafter, he shows a gradual tapering off. In the first six books the frequency is 351 elisions per 1000 lines (all types considered). This is, in fact, more than any other English poet had seen fit to adopt since the final -*e* of Middle English ceased to be treated as a metrical device.[1] In Books VII through XII the average was 279 elisions per 1000 lines. That is substantially the average Milton maintained in *Paradise Regained* (288 per 1000 lines), though in that poem there is, as has been noted, considerable difference among the four books. In *Samson Agonistes* the frequency of metrical elision decreases even further, to 245 per 1000 lines, but there Milton was not faced with exactly the same problems. *Samson* is dramatic verse and required less attention to devices of this nature to prevent monotony. Moreover, in *Samson* Milton did not return to the practice of *Comus;* with regard to the frequency of elision *Samson* is much closer to *Paradise Re-*

---

1. I have treated this matter at some length elsewhere, in "The Theory and Practice of Poetic Elision."

gained and the last half of *Paradise Lost* than it is to *Comus*. And if one were to examine each category of elision in detail in *Samson*, it would quickly be noticed that so far as quality is concerned Milton brings to the dramatic poem all of the skill he showed in *Paradise Lost* plus, in some respects, considerably more daring. He continued to extend the list of words that could enter into elidible situations, but, by and large, where he intended the lines to be decasyllabic, he was as regular in *Samson* as he had been in *Paradise Lost*. This evidence tends to confirm the orthodox chronology of Milton's work (see the Graph on page 67).

There can be little doubt that Milton learned his technique of metrical elision from studying the English poets. But he must also have picked up many pointers from the poetry and handbooks of other languages. Surely, he noted with attentiveness what took place in classical poetry, and there is little reason to doubt that he found something to be learned in Italian poetry and criticism. But, on the whole, his elisions were traditional English varieties, and the bulk of his actual cases were already familiar to him from his reading of English poetry. For example, he made great use of the commonplace synaloephae involving the article, and he also liked *many a*, an elision found frequently in the earlier poets. To the use of elisions based on contiguous vowels he brought great virtuosity, but many of his elisions in this category were not his own inventions. The monosyllabic use of *being*, for example, was almost as common in Marlowe and Shakespeare as it was in Milton.

It is not possible to identify the influences on Milton's metrical technique much more closely than that. A comparison of his elisions with those of other poets indicates that he read and studied all the important poets with close attention. Sometimes one finds an elision in Milton that seems to have come to him from Donne or Shakespeare or Jonson, but there are too few of these for one to generalize about them. On the whole the elisions belonged to everyone; they were part of a metrical tradition on which all the poets could draw (and all the great ones did).

In one respect Milton seems to have adopted a technique directly from Chaucer; that is, the use of both elided and unelided forms in adjacent lines (e.g., *Paradise Lost* III.131-32, III.216-17, or IX.1025-26).

Milton has always been recognized as a great prosodist; indeed he has received more attention in this regard than any other poet in the language. After Bridges' work most students were ready to admit that Milton employed some system of metrical elision, though they were not always willing to agree just what that was. On the whole *Milton's Prosody* (especially since the 1921 edition) has proved convincing if not quite satisfactory. But Bridges did not recognize that Milton's system was an extension and refinement of a strong metrical tradition that had existed for centuries. Bridges believed, but was not always able to persuade his readers to agree, that Milton's system was a conscious technique. Some students still seem to believe that metrical elision, while it exists, is essentially a reflection of a poet's pronunciation under certain circumstances. Nothing could be further from the truth. Even a cursory study of Milton shows how very much aware he was of metrical matters, what refinements he went into with regard to details, how anxious he was to guide the reader with adequate, if not consistent, clues to his prosody so that no one might mis-meter him.

Unfortunately, most of the devices Milton employed to make his elisions received no notice in the critical works of his time, though here and there one finds mention of this or that device, usually in the handbooks on rhetoric. We in the twentieth century have grown out of touch with these techniques, just as we have ceased to recognize the tropes and figures of rhetoric when they appear. It is of course our education that is at fault. Over and over again the poets furnish more than adequate clues to their practice.

The great bulk of Milton's work was done in the traditional English decasyllable. A study of elision indicates that this line was understood by the poets to be of a very high degree of regularity, once the permissible elisions are recognized. It was intended to have ten syllables, though the number might be varied by the addition of a feminine ending and truncated lines (that is, lines with the initial syllable omitted) were sometimes permitted.

49

But the poets on the whole did not permit any extrametrical syllables. They wrote verse of great regularity, though their system permitted a great deal of variation. Elision was primarily a device whereby a poet could secure variation in his lines and thus prevent euphonic monotony. It was also, especially in Milton, a device for securing economy; that is, by clever manipulation of elision a poet could pack his lines with much more meaning than would otherwise be possible. Very generally, then, the extensive system of metrical elision on which the English poets might draw helped them to secure something of the same effect that the inflectional system of Latin provided for the Roman poet. Finally, elision might be used functionally, almost symbolically, to help the poet indicate certain things about particular speakers, or certain passages, in his poem. Milton did not employ these devices in this regard often. In *Paradise Lost,* as we have seen, there are a few passages that indicate he was experimenting with the use of elision to emphasize the euphonic quality of the lines in question. In *Paradise Regained* there is even more reason to believe he was prepared to use elision very subtly to underscore the meaning of the plain words of certain passages. But on the whole Milton used these devices to secure variation, so that *Paradise Lost* is not a monotonous poem to read—he had learned a great deal by reading the *Faerie Queene*—but a very clever symphony of sounds. He also used elisions to pack his lines with meaning. There is scarcely any poetry in English, with the possible exception of Shakespeare's, so filled with matter as Milton's.

APPENDIX

For the reader's convenience in locating the elisions in the text of *Paradise Lost*, they are listed herein in their order of appearance, excepting only multiple occurrences (indicated by number parenthetically) and one or two places where it seemed desirable for clarity to list related forms together. Hypermonosyllables, a category containing very few actual words, are listed according to this principle, but it will be harder to locate these in the text.

The figures may not always agree exactly with those in the tables, though differences are of no statistical importance, for I have considered a few doubtful instances in the tabulation. In cases where there may be a doubt in which category to place an elision, I have usually included it with that type of elision that occurs most frequently. A small number of exceptions to this principle have been permitted (on aesthetic grounds), but normally I have attempted to be as consistent as possible. No deviation from principles affects the frequency per 1000 lines more than a small fraction.

A few ligatured symbols employed by Milton are here represented by *ae, Ae,* or *Oe* (in words like *pandaemonium*). Also, in the appendix Milton's capitals have usually been reduced to lower case letters.

Many times an elision listed here may seem to the reader to be a natural speech form. However, I have not included any instances except those in which an expanded pronunciation occurs elsewhere in Milton, elsewhere in the poets of Renaissance, or, in a very few cases, where such a pronunciation might reasonably be expected by analogy. For example, one might object that the word *natural* normally exists in the flow of speech as a disyllable, as well as a trisyllable, and therefore may not be an elision at all. Milton, however, uses both forms.

BOOK I:

HYPERMONOSYLLABLES: heav'nly (3 times), heav'n(s) (35), power(s) (14), orepowr'd, heaven (2), imbowr, flowr, flowry, towrs (2), towr, ev'n, even, flowers—(total 64).

ELISIONS OVER LIQUIDS AND NASALS: (a) over *-r:* adventrous, spirit(s) (9), weltring, merit, conquerour (2), suffering, sulphurous, glimmering, slumbring, thundring (2), mineral, sufferance (2), sovran (2), ponderous, covering, general(s) (2), hovering, barbarous, wandring (2), emperors, watry, bordring, amorous, offrings, glittering, deliberate, considerate, numerous, wondring, severing—(44); (b) over -*l*: perilous, groveling, innumerable as, immeasurable anon, populous, temple of—(6); over -*n*: prison ordain'd, ev'ning, lik'ning, count'nance, hardning, original, op'ning—(7); (d) over -*m* (very doubtful): ceremony—(1)—(58).

SYNALOEPHAE: th'Aonian, th'upright, th'infernal, glory above, th'ethereal, th'Omnipotent (2), th'utmost, th'Arch-Enemy, the unconquerable, ignominy and, th'excess (2), th'Apostate, th'imbattelld, glory extinct, th'Arch-fiend, th'occasion, many a (3), th'ocean, be it, th'Almighty (2), th'associates, th'oblivious, th'Etrurian, to adore, th'advantage, th'uplifted, th'invisible, sanctuary it, vally of, th'obscene, th'Asphaltick, th'offensive, also against, th'infection, th'Ionian, th'Hesperian, to have (3), th'imperial, sorrow and, th'heroic Marocco or, glory obscur'd, th'arch, th'event, th'abysse, th'ascending, th'Aegaean—(54).

ELISION OVER CONTIGUOUS VOWELS: disobedience, Siloa's, Aonian, impious (3), ethereal (2), hideous (2), tempestuous, myriads (2), mutual, glorious, ruin, mightiest, dubious, suppliant, empyreal, experience, perpetual, mightier (2), being (2), impetuous, satiate, Titanian, unusual, subterranean, glorying, Stygian, celestial, associates, oblivious, liveliest, pernicious, superiour, toward (2), Etrurian, Memphian (2), perfidious, chariot, warriers (2), Lybian, memorial, various (3), promiscuous, opprobrious, Israel (3), Syrian (3), bestial, Sidonian, uxorious, annual, Ezekiel, alienated, odious, Belial (2), atheist, luxurious, riot, loftiest, Ionian, Delphian, Adria, Hesperian, clarions, imperial, meteor, orient, Dorian, experienc't, Ilium, auxiliar, Fontarabbia, followers, inglorious, caelestial, highest,[1] Assyria, Ausonian, Aegaean, industrious, Pandaemonium, worthiest, champions, expatiate, Indian, incorporeal—(101).

NON-SYLLABIC -EST: didst (2), know'st, satst, mad'st, beest, seest (2)—(8).

NON-SYLLABIC FINAL NASALS: fall'n (4), fal'n, ris'n, drivn, reason, chos'n, giv'n (2), grav'n—(12) (and one case that is doubtful: temple in [tεmpl̩əv]).

1. In the case of *highest* the elision is not, strictly speaking, between contiguous vowels but between a diphthong and vowel.

52

CONTRACTIONS: o'rewhelm'd, orepowr'd, e're (for ever), oreblown, i'th', nathless,[2] scap't (for escaped), orethrew, ore (3), 'twixt,[3] o're, scape (for escape) (3)—(16).

BOOK II:

HYPERMONOSYLLABLES: heav'n(s) (63), heavn's, heaven, heavenly, heav'nly (e) (4), showrs, showre, power(s) (13), towrs (3), seven-(fold), overpower, flowers, powerful (2), evil—(94).

ELISION OVER LIQUIDS AND NASALS: (a) over -r: thunderers, ling-ring (2), torturer, torturing, desperate, timorous, bordering (2), vent'rous, conquerour (2), sovran, offerings, preferring,[4] prosperous, must'ring, blustring, pillar of, suffering, dangerous, neighbouring, wandring (5), pondering (2), sov'ranty, tollerable, deliverance, reverence, general (2), spirit(s) (6), lowring, several, adventrous, shuddring, monstrous, labouring, artillery, hov'ring, ingendring, battering, fluttring, faultring, numerous, wondrous, glimmering—(56); (b) over -l: evil and, popular, inutterable and, impenitrable impal'd, distinguishable in, invulnerable in, immeasurably all—(7); (c) over -n: ominous, threatning (2), brightning, count'nance (2), ev'ning, deafning, abominable, op'ning (2), original, weakning—(13)—(76).

SYNALOEPHAE: th'Eternal, th'ascent, th'event, to have, th'other (4), th'ethereal (2), th'Almighty (2), ignominy or, th'assembly (2), continue and, th'inevitable, difficulty or, do I, th'adventure, the highest, glory excites, th'antagonist, hollow abyss, th'Olympian, th'envenom'd, th'Euboic, many a (7), glory and, th'obdured, Damiata and (2), th'effect, th'attempt, th'adventrous, adversary of, th'undaunted, folly and, thee and, th'Artick, fury O, t'whom (2), th'host, th'-unfounded, th'intricate, massie Iron, th'infernal, city or, th'advantage, difficulty and (2), th'utmost, th'empyreal (2)—(61).

ELISION OVER CONTIGUOUS VOWELS: gorgeous, insatiate, celestial, glorious (2), happier (2), inferior, opprobrious, Tartarean, laborious, being (4), perpetual (3), Belial (2), industrious, immediate, ethereal (4), victorious (2), intellectual, doing, hideous (4), am-

2. *Nathless* is really a variant rather than a contraction, but as it appears to be used with the same effect and same purpose as a contraction there seems no reason to complicate matters by adding another very small category. A few other examples are similar.

3. Aphetic forms, by the same virtue, are also not strictly speaking contractions.

4. In this category the elision would seem highly fictive.

brosial (2), conspicuous, mightiest, audience (2), imperial (2), easier (2), orient, champions (2), empyreal (2), toward(s) (5), radiant, Stygian (2), presumptuous, likeliest, Pythian, Olympian, Oealia, Thessalian, Oeta, oblivion, Serbonian, periods, Gorgonian, prodigious, highest (2), aequinoctial, Ethiopian, Cerberean, Calabria, Trinacrian, uglier, scorpions, Caspian, odious, violent, dalliance, voluptuous, bestial, impetuous, chariots, empbryon, materials, ruinous, tumultuous, flying, Arimaspian, various, readiest, following, dubious, emptier—(97).

NON-SYLLABIC -EST: breath'st, know'st, call'st (2), becam'st, took'st, sawst, claim'st, show'st, gav'st, seest—(11).

NON-SYLLABIC FINAL NASALS: fall'n (2), ris'n, driv'n (2), giv'n (2), befalln—(8).

CONTRACTIONS: o're (4), e're (apparently for ever) (2), orewatcht, scape, ore (without apostrophe) (3), o'respread, o'rematcht—(13).

BOOK III:

HYPERMONOSYLLABLES: heav'n(s), (33), heaven(s) (7), heavn, heav'nly (4), flowrie, ev'n, even, power(s)(ful) (11), flour(s)(ie) (4), seav'n (2), seven (2), browre—(70).

ELISIONS OVER LIQUIDS AND NASALS; (a) over -r: sovran (2), Tiresias, utterance, uttering (2), deliv'rance, sufferance, offering, wondring, wondrous (3), general, river of, glittering, blustring, glimmering, neighbouring (2), glistering, wondrously, spirit(s) (8), iron, wandring (2), remembrance, several, cumbrous, reverence—(37); (b) over -l: inimitable on—(1); (c) over -n: count'nance, everthreatning, op'ning—(3)—(43).

SYNALOEPHAE: th'eternal (2), I express, th'Orphean, the Almighty, th'ethereal, also is, justly accuse, shadow of, the other, mercy and (2), glorie excel, th'innumerable, th'incensed, th'unjust, th'Almighty (3), many as, glory abounds, thy humiliation, the effulgence, glorie abides, th'aspiring, only extold, mercie and, pitie enclin(e)(d) (2), th'inroad, transitorie and, glorie or, th'other (2), th'unaccomplisht, th'angelical, many a(n) (3), easie ascent, th'earth (2), th'horizon, vertue even, th'arch-chimic, th'Aequator, body opaque, the aire, th'-Arch-Angel, only evil, onely in, timely interposes, the earth, th'-eliptic—(54).

ELISIONS OVER CONTIGUOUS VOWELS: effluence, ethereal (3), Stygian, Phineus, harmonious, shadiest, celestial (3), irradiate, radiant (4), toward(s) (4), obedience (5), influence, ambrosial, glorious (4), heavier, effectual, disobeying, speediest, victorious, inglorious, filial, enjoying, worthiest, gloriously (2), Elisian, melodious, being, conspicuous, chariot (2), copious, inferior, Indian, Elysium, embryos, idiots, devious, orient, guardians, mysteriously, Arabian, Hesperian, various (3), Proteus, vertuous, terrestrial, visual, tiar, illustrious, Uriel (2), likeliest, empyreal, worthiest, material, superior— (76).

NON-SYLLABIC -EST: hear'st, didst (3), revisit'st, know'st, canst (2), sit'st, shad'st, drov'st, seest (2)—(13).

NON-SYLLABIC FINAL NASALS: givn (2), fall'n (2), drivn—(5).

CONTRACTIONS: o're (6).

BOOK IV:

HYPERMONOSYLLABLES: heav'n(s) (29), heaven (2), heav'nl(y)-(ie) (4), towrs, towre, power(s) (9), powerful, powrd, showrd, flour(s)(e) (9), bowrs, bower (4), flowers, shower(s)(d) (3), lours, seavenfold, eeven—(70).

ELISIONS OVER LIQUIDS AND NASALS: (a) over -r: sufferings, remembrance, verdurous, general (3), neighbouring, odoriferous, odorous (3), wandring (2), murmuring (3), gathring, clustring, whispering, savourie, numerous, conquering, utterance, wondring, watry (2), answering (2), amorous, slumbrous, glistring (2), glittering, ministring, sovran, adulterous, ivorie, ingendring, spirit(s) (7), spiritual (2)—(47); (b) over -l: devillish, purple and, devilish, inviolable, violate—(5); (c) over -n: threatning, eminent, gardning, sharpning —(4)—(56).

SYNALOEPHAE: th'Apocalyps, the inhabitants, th'accuser, to accuse, th'Omnipotent, th'Assyrian, many a (3), th'ascent, th'other (2), th'arch-fellon, the East, worthy of, onely and, th'Eternal (2), th'inspired, th'earth, th'unwieldy, unweildy elephant, th'ocean, th'-ascending, continue and, th'expanse, th'Angelic (2), th'unarmed, th'Almighties, th'East, th'hour, body or, beauty adornd, only enlighten, the unwiser, be it, th'accustomd, fancie and, th'animal, vertue in, th'esteem, military obedience, th'acknowledg'd, th'infernal —(45).

ELISIONS OVER CONTIGUOUS VOWELS: furious, tumultuous, towards

(2), meridian (2), glorious (3), easiest, highest, inferio(u)r (2), heavier (2), Uriel (3), Assyrian (2), loftiest, stateliest, goodliest (2), Media, substantial, Seleucia, ambrosial, orient (2), curious, various (3), amiable, Hesperian, irriguous, umbrageous, luxuriant, Libyan, Ethiop, filial, mysterious (3), happiest (3), lovliest, dalliance, Gordian, mutual (3), obedience (3), following (2), happier (3), unexperienc't, being, individual, superior, envious, likelier, conspicuous, Gabriel (6), celestial (4), diamond, impetuous, alien, warriour (2), spiritual (2), earliest (2), echoing, beauteous, costliest, shadier, connubial, bestial, holiest, perpetual, Patriarchs, casual, shaddowie, issuing, Uzziel, radiant, Ithuriel, contemptuous, presumptuous, inexperience, easier, violence, scorpion—(109).

NON-SYLLABIC -EST: look'st, hadst (4), had'st, knowst (5), cryd'st, seest (2), fli'st (2), sitst, telst, bidst, mad'st, com'st, satst, stood'st, resembl'st, wouldst (2), mightst, incurr'st, couldst, fledst, draw'st—(31).

NON-SYLLABIC FINAL NASALS: unshak'n, giv'n (3), forbidd'n, fall'n, ris'n, chos'n, driv'n—(9).

CONTRACTIONS: sdeind, o're (6), oreleapt, scap't, scape—(10).

BOOK V:
HYPERMONOSYLLABLES: heav'n(s) (42), heaven(s) (2), heav'nly (4), power(s) (17), pow'r, showers, showrd, towrs (2), towring, flours (2), floure, flower, flouring, flourets, bowre (4), dowr, eeven, ev'n, even (2), seaventimes—(87).

ELISIONS OVER LIQUIDS AND NASALS: (a) over -r: temperat, whispering, wondring (2), ventrous, (un)savourie (3), wandring, arborous, hov'ring, discovering, numerous (2), wondrous (2), sov'ran (2), glittering (2), nectarous, reverence, several (2), differing, corporal (2), surety, neighbouring, innumerable, sovran, remembrest, rememberest, sanctuarie, dextrous—(35); (b) over -l: inextricable or—(1); (c) over -n: gard'n of, ris'n on, disburd'ning, unlibidinous, lik'ning, awak'ning, count'nance, light'ning, quick'ning—(9)—(45).

SYNALOEPHAE: th'eastern (2), th'only, envie or, we affirm, the earth, the uncolourd, th'adopted, th'Eternal (2), th'angelic (3), th'empyreal (3), to all, many a, berrie and, to a, two onely, the angelic, to entertain, no ingrateful, the empiric, to have (2), th'occasion, me and, journey and, me O, th'invisible, shaddow of, to other, th'Almight(y)(ies) (2), into utter, th'Omnipotent, we have, th'all, the unsleeping, envie against, th'unwarie, to erect, th'abuse, deitie and, glory &, th'incensed (2), th'Apostat, th'anointed—(51).

ELISIONS OVER CONTIGUOUS VOWELS: orient (2), shadowie, ambrosia (1) (3), happier, worthier, various (6), glorious (5), quaternion, perpetual, melodious (2), bounteous, Raphael (2) violence, celestial (3), empyreal (3), ethereal (3), Cassia, superfluous, juciest, kindliest, India, superior (3), meridian, spiritual (3), corporeal, mellifluous, transubstantiate, drossiest, being (5), radiant, gradual, intellectual, diet, obedient (2), patriarch, (dis)obedience (5), delineate, imperial (2), hierarch(al)(ies) (3), memorials, individual, bounteous, copious, roseat, friendliest, contemptuous, myriads, shadowie, associate, ambiguous, diamond, calumnious, audience, Abdiel (2), impious (2), experience, illustrious, alienate, perfidious—(97).

NON-SYLLABIC -EST: sleepst (2), mayst, canst (2), didst (3), sitst, crownst, climb'st, fallst, meetst, fli'st, hear'st, find'st, couldst, continu'st, tellst, injoinst, seest, laugh'st, saist (2)—(24).

NON-SYLLABIC FINAL NASALS: risen, falln, fall'n (2), given, giv'n (2)—(7).

CONTRACTIONS: o're (2), scap't, submiss, oreshades, twixt—(6).

BOOK VI:

HYPERMONOSYLLABLES: heav'n(s) (52), heaven, power(s) (17), heavenl(y)(ie) (3), overpowerd, powerfullest, towring, showr, showrie, flour, flourets, eevn—(81).

ELISIONS OVER LIQUIDS AND NASALS: (a) over -r: sovran, advent'rous, innumerable, inconquerable, ministring (2), spirit(s) (5), encountring, numerous (2), entring, nectarous, wondrous (2), answering (2), deliverer, deliverance, thundring, thunderer, dolorous, neighbouring, sanctuarie, dangerous, bickering, timerous, monstrous, measuring—(32); (b) over -l: evil unknown, invulnerable impenitrably, dev'lish, devilish, devillish, invisible is—(6); over -n: streit'ning, op'ning (2), count'nance—(4)—(42).

SYNALOEPHAE: testimonie of, many a(n) (4), th'horizon, th'Eternal (2), th'apostat, th'Almightie('s) (2), th'Omnipotent, th'unwise, th'Arch-angel, armie against, the arch, th'angelic (2), to Almightie, th'ethereal, many and, glorie aspires, th'inviolable, th'other (2), th'assembly, th'invention, th'inventer, easie it, th'originals, easie and, to

57

oppose, th'assessor, vertue and, glorie account, th'undying, th'impure, the uprooted, th'obdurate, t'whom, th'accurst, th'unsufferable, th'explusion, to have—(44).

ELISIONS OVER CONTIGUOUS VOWELS: perpetual (2), obsequious (2), empyreal (2), orient (2), chariot(s)(er) (12), myriads, mightier, easier, glorious (2), Michael (5), celestial (4), Gabriel (2), ethereal (2), obvious, various (2), furious (2), envier, hideous (3), Abdiel (3), mightiest (5), highest (2), erroneous, dieties, worthiest (4), worthier, impious (2), saying, warriour (2), plenteous, heaviest, easier, imperious, conspicuous, discontinuous, issuing, memorial, bellowing, Uriel, diamond, atheist, Ariel, Arioc, Ramiel, oblivion, ignominious, disobedience (3), violence, odious, superiour, ethereous, ambrosial, materials, beauteous, ambient, infuriate, mutual, arguing, speediest, Zophiel, flying, shaddowing (2), ambiguous, immediate, impetuous, Belial, shadowing, likeliest, filial, holiest, gladlier, obedience (2), radiant, illustrious, contiguous, tempestuous, victorious—(121).

NON-SYLLABIC -EST: didst, seest (3), returnst, comst, errst, deprav'st, dar'st, saidst, canst, shouldst, call'st, believst, knowst, seekst, declarst, lov'st, hat'st, maist (2)—(21).

NON-SYLLABIC FINAL NASALS: fall'n (2), giv'n (2), prison—(5).

CONTRACTIONS: gan, 'twixt, orewearied, orewhelm, o're (2)—(6).

BOOK VII:

HYPERMONOSYLLABLES: heav'n(s) (37), heaven, heav'nl(y)(ie) (4), power(s) (3), powerful, flour'd, towre, eev'n (3), ev'n (2), evil (2), seaventh, seav'nth—(57).

ELISIONS OVER LIQUIDS AND NASALS: (a) over -r: tempring, barbarous, wandring (2), differing, sovran, temperance, spirit(s) (5), several, clustring, luminaries, numerous (2), innumerous, pasturing, liveries, wondrous, answering—(22); (b) over -l: unimaginable as, innumerable and, communicable in, immeasurable abyss—(4); (c) over -n: listning (2), soft'ning, op'ning (2)—(5)—(31).

SYNALOEPHAE: th'Olympian, th'Almight(y)(ie)('s) (4), th'Aleian, timely of, the infinitly, th'invisible, folly as, th'Omnipotent, th'ungodly, th'habitations, the Armoury, th'Omnific, th'abyss, vertue infus'd, th'earth (3), the humble, the earth (4), th'expanse, to illuminate, th'horizon, the op'n, unweildie enormous, the egg, th'air, th'other, starrie eyes, azure and, the Omnipotent, the Aire, th'addition, th'impereal—(39).

ELISIONS OVER CONTIGUOUS VOWELS: Urania (2), following, Olympian, celestial (4), empyreal, Aleian, erroneous, narrower, audience (2), conspicuous, ambient, illustrious, happier, victorious, envious, obedience (2), overshadowing, filial (2), immediate, hierarchies, radiance, radiant, sapience, chariot(s) (2), myriads, spontaneous, harmonious, furious, tartareous, ethereal (2), orient, circumfluous, contiguous, embryon, satiate, immediately, perpetual, various, copious, glorious (2), borrowing, dividual, plenteously, saying, wallowing, mutual, annual, clarion, ambiguous, sinuous, parsimonious, varietie, symphonious, impereal, impiously—(65).

NON-SYLLABIC -EST: dwell'st, didst, visit'st, maist, canst, knowst (3), gav'st, suttl'st, becam'st, mai'st, eat'st, di'st, remember'st, heard'st, seest, creat'st, seek'st—(19).

NON-SYLLABIC FINAL NASALS: fall'n (2), driv'n—(3).

No CONTRACTIONS.

BOOK VIII:
HYPERMONOSYLLABLES: heav'n(s) (22), heav'nl(y)(ie) (8), power (3), powerful, overpowerd, flour(s) (3), flourie, bowers, boure, bowre, sev'nth, eev'n—(44).

ELISIONS OVER LIQUIDS AND NASALS: (a) over -r: entring, wondrous, glistering, luminaries, spiritual, wandring (3), different (2), several, sufferance, remembrance, sovran (2), wondring, endevoring, murmuring, watry, cowring, ordering, solitarie, collateral, spirit(s) (4), amorous, honouring, higher in—(30); (b) over -l: invisible else, innumerable ordain'd—(2); (c) over -n: reasoning (2), count'nance, luminous, discount'nanc't, reason and, condescension and —(7)—(39).

SYNALOEPHAE: to ask, the eye, me &, th'Almighty, the highth, to his, th'inferiour, occasionally and, the eare, I approve, onely or, happie and (2), body enjoy'st—(14).

ELISIONS OVER CONTIGUOUS VOWELS: hystorian, officiate, punctual, superfluous, (in)corporeal (2), studious, gladlier, mutual (2), Raphael (2), spiritual, various(ly) (4), industrious, transpicuous, terrestrial, obvious (2), being (3), easiest, easier, experience, satiate,

59

toward, obedience (2), furious, happier, goodliest, higher, presumptuous, inferiour (3), tedious, associates, deficience, celestial (2), glorious, bounteous, enviest, obsequious, superiour, vertuousest, loveliest, mysterious, harmonious, irradiance, virtual, immediate, Hesperean, ethereal—(59).

NON-SYLLABIC -EST: supposest, thinkst (2), seest (4), soughst, eat'st, call'st, know'st (3), shouldst (2), seek'st, canst, spak'st, saw'st, could'st, need'st, perceav'st, admir'st, maist (2), blam'st, saist, enjoy'st—(28).

NON-SYLLABIC FINAL NASALS: giv'n (2).

CONTRACTIONS: o're (2), oreflow'd, e're (for ever), submiss—(5).

BOOK IX:

HYPERMONOSYLLABLES: heav'n(s) (16), heav'nl(y)(ie) (5), pow'r, power(s) (8), powerful, flour(s) (9), flourie, deflourd, bowers, bowre (2), tour'd, imbowr'd, lowr'd, seven, eevn, even, evil (6)— (57).

ELISIONS OVER LIQUIDS AND NASALS: (a) over -r: slumbring, concentring, centring, maistring, azure or, sovran (4), savorie (2), wandring (2), wandering, spirit(s) (2), hovering, wondrous, ventring, reverence, faultring, adventrous, liberal, muttering, amorous, utterance, pasturing, covering—(28); (b) over -l: populous, informidable exempt, capitoline, articulat, credulous—(5); (c) over -n: gardning (2), reasoning (2), reason and, threatner, eat'n and, opener, countnance, threatening—(10)—(43).

SYNALOEPHAE: the horizon, the eighth, vertue appeers, me as, the infernal, th'angelic, he effected, many a (3), th'approach, th'earths, th'hour, th'attempt (2), though in, th'assault, the influence, th'event (2), th'other (2), dairie each, enemie of, beautie adore, thee and, he obeyd, th'amaz'd, to excess, th'offence, be admired, bodie and, th'effects, enemie hath, to incurr, so oft, th'American, to approve, to have, th'accuser, to her—(41).

ELISIONS OVER CONTIGUOUS VOWELS: venial, disobedience, alienated, Lavinia, celestial (2), studious, Gabriel, heavier, Uriel, worthier, terrestrial (2), gradual, (in)glorious (3), highest, bestial, intelligential, luxurious, casual, associate, lovelier (2), (in)satiate (3), societie, envying (2), being (3), (un)seemliest (2), inffectual, superfluous, matrimonial, exterior, obedience, towards, patriarch,

Oread, likeliest, stateliest, sapien(t)(ce) (3), dalliance (2), issuing, intellectual (2), Illyria, Ammonian, Olympias, Scipio, tortuous, duteous, various, fluctuats, audience, happier, easier, vertuous (2), experience (2), following, continual, superior (2), inferior, ambrosial, odious, deitie, amiable, illustrious, lascivious, mutual (2), Herculean, Indian(s) (2), echoing, Amazonian, sensual—(88).

NON-SYLLABIC -EST: receav'st, knowst, shouldst (4), fearst, wouldst (2), seemst, foundst, canst (2), cam'st, command'st, op'nst, giv'st, saidst (2), didst (4), hadst (3), imput'st, call'st, could'st—(29).

NON-SYLLABIC FINAL NASALS: giv'n, given, driv'n, befall'n, forbidd'n, forbidden—(6).

CONTRACTIONS: twixt, submiss, 'gan—(3).

BOOK X:

HYPERMONOSYLLABLES: heav'n(s) (18), heaven (3), heav'nly (3), power(s) (16), powerful, impow'rd, showre, bowrs, flour(s) (2), seav'n, eevn, devil,[5] evill—(50).

ELISIONS OVER LIQUIDS AND NASALS: (a) over -r: wondring (2), whether in,[6] collateral, faultring, sovran, adventrous, savour of, hovering, wondrous (2), sev'ral, several (2), dang'rous, numerous, emperour, adventurer, accessories, spattering, conquering, thundrous, lateral, miserie, natural, spirit, thundring, incorporate, wandring, reverence, recovering, shivering, labouring, shattering, watering (2)—(36); (b) over -l: groveling, idlely, innumerable and, obicular, abominable accurst, tollerable and, Serraliona, miserable of, miserable it—(9); (c) over -n: discount'nanc't, garden and, opening, ravenous (2), listning, unoriginal, bituminous, count'nance, reasonings, begotten and, rav'nous—(12)—(57).

SYNALOEPHAE: to have (2), th'angelic, th'unwelcome, th'ethereal, thee and, mercie as, glorie him, deitie erewhile, to offend, obstinacie and, thou art, thee above, th'accus'd, thou hast, thy wife,[7] also and,

---

5. *Devil* like *evil* is an exceptional hypermonosyllable; it did, however, have a monosyllabic pronunciation in some dialects.
6. In a few cases before Milton *whether* appears to have been used as a hypermonosyllable itself.
7. Elisions of this nature, in which the word ending in a vowel precedes a semivowel rather than another vowel or aspirate are extremely rare in Milton.

th'herb, th'instant, difficultie of, th'infernal (2), many a (3), th' imagin'd, th'indignant, to observe, vertue hath, fully aveng'd, th'empyreal, th'affaires, th'other (2), the inland, th'upper, th'acclaime, onely of, to our, my adventure, th'unreal, th'untractable, fiercely oppos'd, to increase, th'account, th'open, th'applause, th'offended, they assayd, th'equinoctial, th'horizon, th'irrational, alreadie in, sorrow abandoned, happie is, glory who, thou enjoy, me I, thee of, justly is, be it (2), th'extent, happie had, vertu all, adversarie his, onely I, unwarie and, thee I, pitie incline, th'inclement, sorrow unfeign'd (2)—(73).

ELISIONS OVER CONTIGUOUS VOWELS: celestial, ethereal, toward(s) (4), immediate (2), radiant, obvious, conspicuous, being (3), superior, vitiated, mysterious, saying, pittying, opprobrious, happier, impervious, following (4), Cronian, Gorgonian, Memnonian, Asia,[8] scorpion (2), various (2), stupendious, illustrious, alienated, empyreal, glorious (4), associate, issuing (3), Pandaemonium, Bactrian, Plutonian, Stygian, inferiour, Pythian, annual, actual, habitual, plenteous, incestuous, victorious, audience, extenuate, solstitial, tempestuous, equinoctial, perpetual, Thyestean, Boreas, Caecias, Thrascias, Libecchio, gloomiest, disobedient, corporeal, heavier (2), Happiest, cruel, erroneous, easier, wiselier, highest, piteous, pitying, commodiously, humiliation (2)—(86).

NON-SYLLABIC -EST: mayst, knowst (2), shouldst, wouldst (2), mad'st, gav'st, didst (4), did'st, had'st, view'st, hadst, thinkst, wouldst, couldst, desir'st (2), fearst, feelst, bearst—(24).

NON-SYLLABIC FINAL NASALS: stoln, fall'n (3), driv'n (4), giv'n (3), ris'n (2), befall'n (2), forgiv'n, light'n—(17).

CONTRACTIONS: scape, gan—(2).

BOOK XI:

HYPERMONOSYLLABLES: heav'n(s) (18), heavn, heavn's, heav'nly (5), power(s) (4), powre, bowrs, bowre, flour(s) (3), flourie, showr, towrs, ev'n, eev'n (3), seventh, seavens, evil—(45).

ELISIONS OVER LIQUIDS AND NASALS: (a) over -r: regenerate, spirit(s) (5), general, sovran, pastoral, reverence (3), glistering,

---

8. Though *Asia* with disyllabic value may seem unlikely to be an elision, it occurs elsewhere as a trisyllable, particularly in the verse of Marlowe.

recovering (2), whether among,[9] suffering(s) (2), different (2), offring, offering, (in)temperance (4), monstrous, feavorous, disfiguring, connatural, combrous, rendring, labouring, iron, neighbouring, amorous (2), mustring, batterie, sulfurous, reverend, hovering, numerous, wandring, watrie (2), degenerate, wondrous— (48); (b) over -*l:* variable and, inhospitable appeer, jav'lin—(3); (c) over -*n:* cov'nant (2), op'ning (2), count'nance, praeeminence, chast'ning, original, resonant, opener, effeminate, threatning, betok'ning, covenant—(14)—(65).

SYNALOEPHAE: th'ancient, th'angelic, th'Almighty, th'unholie, th'archangelic, th'offended, to entitle, th'eastern, th'air, to offend, th'Arch-angel (2), th'ambrosial, onely his, th'earth (3), many a, the hand, th'empire, th'effects, th'excepted, th'Angel (4), t'whom, th'unjust, th'others, th'entrance, th'inabstinence, th'image, the harp, th'eevning, to admit, pittie and, th'ensanguind, bodie or, be admir'd, sorrow a, heav'nly instructer—(41).

ELISIONS OVER CONTIGUOUS VOWELS: lowliest, speedier, Deucalion, envious, propitiation, toward(s) (3), unharmonious, happier, Michael (11), warriours (2), perpetual, sorrowing, easiest (2), Arcadian, opiate, Leucothea, deitie, laborious, goodliest, orient, radiant, glorious, guardians, Syrian, celestial (3), livelier, Zodiac, ambrosial, highest, assiduous, virtual, following, obvious, higher, mightiest, visual, ingredients, violent (3), pietie (2), immediately, busiest, various, melodious, casual, studious, beauteous, atheists, superiour, rightlier, odious, marrying, impetuous, being, luxurious, furious, conspicuous, violence—(76).

NON-SYLLABIC -EST: didst (2), may'st, mayst (3), maist, know'st, wak'st, slepst, lead'st, saw'st (3), eatst, drinkst, livst, beheldst (2), stoodst, utterdst, canst, aim'st,—(23).

NON-SYLLABIC FINAL NASALS: fall'n (2), stol'n, giv'n (2), befall'n, grav'n, burd'n, drivn—(9).

CONTRACTIONS: wherere, o're (2), ope (for open), Ith'—(5).

BOOK XII:
HYPERMONOSYLLABLES: heav'n(s) (23), heav'nly, power(s) (7), powrd, bowre, showre, tower (2), towre, towrs, seaven (2), seventie—(41).

9. As previously noted *whether* may also be a monosyllable, in Chaucer, for instance.

ELISIONS OVER LIQUIDS AND NASALS: (a) over -*r:* labouring, wine-offerings, sovrantie, spirit(s) (9), cumbrous, numerous (2), wandring (3), neighbouring, deliverer (2), wondrous (2), pillar of (2), entring, deliverance (2), sanctuary, natural (2), remembring, suffering (2), temporal, spiritual (2), slandrous, labourers, temperate, lingring—(41); (b) over -*l:* ridiculous, temple enshrine, popular, temple itself, answerable add—(5); (c) over -*n:* bituminous, original, cov'nant (3), op'ning, hastning—(7)—(53).

SYNALOEPHAE: the Archangel (3), citie &, th'irreverent, inhospitably and, glory and, th'Egyptian, th'earth, th'obdurst, citie his, hereditarie and, many as, to appeer, glory and, th'unfaithful (2), th'angel (2), to evangelize, to avail, th'ethereal, also in, sorrow and, th'eastern—(25).

ELISIONS OVER CONTIGUOUS VOWELS: audience, plenteous, towards, various (2), hideous, Michael (3), dividual, being (2), immediately, violent, patriar(k)(ch) (2), plainlier, chariot, readiest, (in)glorious (2), mediator, Messiah, obedien(t)(ce) (4), Zodiac, Gibeon, Israel, shadowie (2), filial, Joshua, steddiest, deadlier, profluent, happier (3), period, followers, spiritual (3), amplier, higher, ethereal, Libyan—(49).

NON-SYLLABIC -EST: abhorr'st, canst (2), saw'st, didst, shouldst, knowst, enjoydst,[10] returnst, wentst[11]—(10).

NON-SYLLABIC FINAL NASALS: giv'n (4), given, ris'n—(6).

CONTRACTIONS: stablisht (for established), o're—(2).

10. In a very few words in which the vowel of -*est* inflection has been syncopated a -*d* may be inserted, either by some process of assimilation or perhaps simply as a spelling error.

11. *Wentest,* though an unusual form, also occurs in *Paradise Regained,* IV.

TABLE 1

ELISIONS IN *PARADISE LOST*

ACTUAL NUMBER

Book	I	II	III	IV	V	VI	VII	VIII	IX	X	XI	XII
Hypermonosyllables	64	94	70	70	87	81	57	44	57	50	45	41
Elis. over Liq. & Nasals	58	76	43	56	45	42	31	39	43	57	65	53
Synaloephae	54	61	54	45	51	44	39	14	41	73	41	25
Elis. over Cont. vowels	101	97	76	109	97	121	65	59	88	86	76	49
Non-syllabic -*est*	8	11	13	31	24	21	19	28	29	24	23	10
Non-syllabic final nasals	12	8	5	9	7	5	3	2	6	17	9	6
Contractions	16	13	6	10	6	6	0	5	3	2	5	2
Freq. All Elis.	313	360	267	330	317	320	214	191	267	309	264	186

A few extremely doubtful cases have been omitted.

TABLE 2

FREQUENCY OF ELISIONS PER 1000 LINES IN *PARADISE LOST*

Book	I	II	III	IV	V	VI	VII	VIII	IX	X	XI	XII
Hypermonosyllables	80	89	94	70	96	90	89	68	48	45	50	63
Elis. over Liq. & Nasals	73	72	59	55	49	46	49	60	36	52	72	82
Synaloephae	68	57	73	44	56	48	61	22	34	66	45	39
Elis. over Cont. vowels	126	92	97	107	107	133	101	91	74	78	85	76
Non-syllabic -*est*	10	10	18	31	27	23	33	43	24	22	26	15
Non-syllabic final nasals	15	8	7	9	8	5	5	3	5	15	10	9
Contractions	20	12	8	10	7	7	0	8	2	2	5	3
Freq. All Elis.	391	341	360	325	351	351	334	293	225	279	293	287

A few extremely doubtful cases have been omitted.

65

TABLE 3
ELISIONS IN *PARADISE REGAINED*
ACTUAL NUMBER AND FREQUENCY PER 1000 LINES

Book	I		II		III		IV	
	No.	Freq.	No.	Freq.	No.	Freq.	No.	Freq.
Hypermonosyllables	33	66	13	27	14	32	22	34
Elis. over Liq. & Nasals	18	36	27	58	29	65	27	42
Synaloephae	24	48	20	41	27	61	26	41
Elis. over Cont. vowels	38	76	37	76	60	135	63	100
Non-syllabic -*est*	17	34	20	41	20	45	31	49
Non-syllabic final nasals	6	12	3	6	2	4	4	6
Contractions	11	22	1	2	3	7	1	2
Total Elis.	147		121		155		174	
Freq. All Elis.		280		249		350		272

TABLE 4
ELISIONS IN *COMUS* AND *SAMSON AGONISTES*
ACTUAL NUMBER AND FREQUENCY PER 1000 LINES

	Comus		Samson Agonistes	
	No.	Freq.	No.	Freq.
Hypermonosyllables	25	32	28	23
Elis. over Liq. & Nasals	49	62	67	54
Synaloephae	19	24	68	55
Elis. over Cont. Vowels	34	43	84	68
Non-syllabic -*est*	10	13	44	36
Non-syllabic final nasals	1	—	11	8
Total Elis.	143[1]		302	
Freq. All Elis.		182		245

[1] A small number of contractions have been included in the total.

GRAPH
Number of Elisions per 1,000 Lines

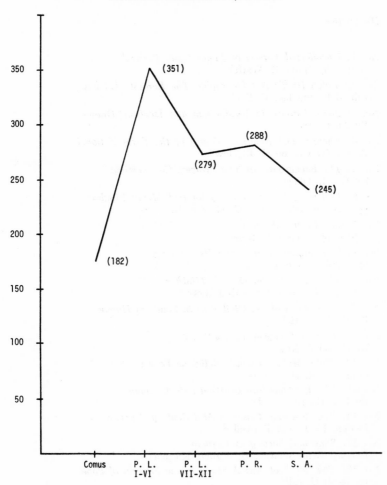

UNIVERSITY OF FLORIDA MONOGRAPHS

Humanities

8-403